Proven Marketing Tips for the Successful Cat Breeder

Volume 1 in the Felines by Design Series

by Jasmine Kinnear
Successful Cat Breeder,
Feline Behavior Consultant and
Cattery Management & Marketing Mentor

CCB Publishing
British Columbia, Canada

Proven Marketing Tips for the Successful Cat Breeder

Copyright ©2006 by Jasmine Kinnear
ISBN-10   0-9739050-6-9
ISBN-13   978-0-9739050-6-9
First Edition

Library and Archives Canada Cataloguing in Publication

Kinnear, Jasmine, 1953-
Proven marketing tips for the successful cat breeder / Jasmine Kinnear.
(Felines by design series ; v. 1)
ISBN 0-9739050-6-9
1. Cats--Marketing. 2. Cats--Breeding. I. Title. II. Series: Kinnear, Jasmine, 1953- Felines by design series ; v. 1
SF442.7.K56 2006   636.7'0887'0688   C2006-900175-8

Extreme care has been taken to ensure that all information presented in this book is accurate and up to date at the time of publishing. Neither the author nor the publisher can be held responsible for any errors or omissions. Additionally, neither is any liability assumed for damages resulting from the use of the information contained herein.

All rights reserved. No part of this publication may be reproduced, stored in a retrieval system or transmitted in any form or by any means, electronic, mechanical, photocopying, recording or otherwise without the express written permission of the publisher. Printed in the United States of America and the United Kingdom.

Publisher: CCB Publishing
              British Columbia, CANADA
              e-mail: info@confessionsofacatbreeder.com

Web site

www.confessionsofacatbreeder.com

PROVEN MARKETING TIPS FOR THE SUCCESSFUL CAT BREEDER
VOLUME 1 IN THE FELINES BY DESIGN SERIES

Table of Contents

Title Page	....	1
Table of Contents	....	3
Dedication	....	5
Introduction	....	7
Who is Jasmine Kinnear?	....	9
Jasmine's Story	....	10
Testimonials	....	14
Jasmine's Jewels of Wisdom	....	16
The Soul of a Breeder	....	16
A Cattery of Substance	....	17
A Breeder of Substance	....	17
Finding a Mentor	....	18
Jasmine's Confession of Finding Her Mentor	....	23
How to Advertise Your Cattery	....	32
Promoting Your Cattery	....	38

PROVEN MARKETING TIPS FOR THE SUCCESSFUL CAT BREEDER
VOLUME 1 IN THE FELINES BY DESIGN SERIES

Promoting Yourself	43
Some Essential Questions for Breeders	45
Helpful Cat Show Hints	57
As Jasmine Says…	58
Successful and Proven Selling Techniques	60
Pictures, Pictures, Pictures!	64
The Compassionate Breeder	66
Breeding Schedule	69
Jasmine's List of Absolute Do's and Don'ts	71
Absolute Do's	71
Still More Absolute Do's	75
Absolute Don'ts	78
Conclusion	82
Bonnie's Story	82
Jasmine's Response	83
Publications & Services from Jasmine Kinnear	85
How to Contact Jasmine Kinnear	86
Glossary of Breeder Jargon Including Many More Breeding Tips from Jasmine	87
Notes	110

PROVEN MARKETING TIPS FOR THE SUCCESSFUL CAT BREEDER
VOLUME 1 IN THE FELINES BY DESIGN SERIES

Dedication

This book is dedicated with love to my mother Ruth.

Thank you for your financial assistance in purchasing Chantal and Tara my first two breeding felines.

Love,

Jasmine

PROVEN MARKETING TIPS FOR THE SUCCESSFUL CAT BREEDER
VOLUME 1 IN THE FELINES BY DESIGN SERIES

Introduction

Whether as a novice or an established cattery it becomes necessary to distinguish yourself from the many catteries in your breeding area. **Proven Marketing Tips for the Successful Cat Breeder** is a valuable insider's guide to promoting your cattery and achieving success within the closed Cat Fancy World. These valuable marketing secrets will provide many unique ideas which will soon have other breeders taking notice. You will leave your competition at a loss by your newly acquired breeding and marketing skills. This publication will aid you in making your cattery both a productive and successful one.

As you read this book you will discover that my approach differs from those found in other cat breeding books. I have not attempted to produce an encyclopedic list of the many breeds of felines available for sale in the world. Many other authors have already completed this task. Instead I have assembled a combination of intriguing and useful facts. You will also discover seldom revealed secrets acquired from my two decades of experience in breeding, selling, and the study of behavior in felines.

This is the first volume in the **Felines by Design** series. It is an uplifting, spiritual and inspiring journey of discovery that will guide you through the Cat Fancy World and beyond.

Whether as a breeder or purebred kitten buyer you will gain insight and strength through this series of publications. A successful breeder for over 20 years, these truly are **Confessions of a Cat Breeder.**

> **When you love what you do, positive energy will be projected and you will attract success.**

A cattery will be a success when the breeder truly loves her cats.

No matter where you are in the world, sound marketing principles cannot be taken for granted when you have the desire to excel as a breeder. The value in purchasing this publication is in the future success of your cattery business.

There are cat lovers and cat breeders. A buyer can tell the difference. A good breeder is both.

Please refer to the **Glossary of Breeder Jargon** at the conclusion of this book. You will find the information quite useful when communicating with established breeders and in the daily operation of your cattery. You may also discover a few jewels of wisdom.

Who Is Jasmine Kinnear?

When Jasmine began her cattery the closed society of breeders in her area would not share information. Despite contacting a number of breeders she was prevented from purchasing cats to use within her breeding program. She was forced to search elsewhere and learned through trial and error how to successfully buy, breed and sell purebred felines. It then became a journey of discovery combining time with knowledge as her teacher. With some experience Jasmine soon realized there was a knack to bringing back buyers, their family members and many more referrals.

Through years of breeding she gained an expertise learning how to professionally breed and sell kittens. Eventually she gained the respect of the veterinarian community to become a top breeder and the most respected in her area.

As her reputation for success grew Jasmine was continuously contacted by the very same breeders who had previously refused to assist her. Word spread to the other catteries of the marketing secrets she developed which resulted in her cattery becoming a profitable business. Her breeding program progressed to the point whereby her litters were sold up to a year prior to their conception. She encountered many anxious breeders hungry for the same success within their own catteries. These breeders also wanted a good income and a proven breeding program. Jasmine's recipe for success is managing a cattery where the breeder incorporates strong ethics with sound business practices.

Jasmine's Story

I lived alone in total harmony with two devoted domestic male cats. With time, as my males aged, I became anxious to purchase a purebred female kitten. However I was quite ignorant of the many breeds of felines available. Worse still, I was unaware of the dynamics I would create by becoming a multi-cat household living within a limited space. Nevertheless like many others driven by a strong case of 'kitten fever' I ignored my good instincts.

For weeks I frantically searched the ads in my local newspaper until one finally appeared for persian / himalayan kittens. At the time I'd never heard of this type of purebred and had little idea of what I would be encountering. In my initial contact by telephone, the breeder seemed preoccupied and was reluctant to answer even a few simple questions.

The only cattery I viewed was this same breeder's small, cramped home where several litters were confined to a minuscule area in her kitchen. Her stud cats were kept out of sight but their presence was clearly evident by the heavily scented odor of spraying males. The breeder had been impatient and indifferent when I spoke to her earlier by phone. During the time I spent with her this attitude only continued as she answered additional telephone inquiries while I viewed the kittens.

Despite her manner, I knew from the first moment I entered her cattery that I would one day become a breeder myself. Although I had just realized my true calling it was an additional ten years before my dream became a reality.

I now realize that many breeders believe sales are only accomplished when a buyer is within their cattery. This is simply untrue. It was my experience that my litters were sold because the buyer's welfare was one of my main priorities. It was important to not only listen but to educate with sound practical advice when the buyer displayed an interest in learning. I enjoyed interacting with other cat lovers and they appreciated that I sincerely enjoyed listening to their feline experiences.

The buyer developed a personal interest in my cattery by establishing a genuine and warm relationship in the initial telephone contact. The perspective buyer then desired to view my cattery and to exchange additional feline anecdotes with a caring breeder. By displaying an interest in their situation before I actually met them it became apparent that many of my kittens were sold by simply listening to the buyer's needs.

Buyers love to share their personal feline experiences. It can be a valuable tool in promoting your cattery if you invest some time and have a sincere interest in a buyer's situation. When you develop good listening skills you will also attract sales. I learned the initial investment of my personal time with telephone inquiries became a key component to the volume of sales within my cattery.

As a naïve buyer sitting in Theresa's cattery kitchen I questioned her regarding my living conditions with two male cats. I was renting a one bedroom apartment and didn't know what to expect if I brought a female home. The breeder reassured me that despite my limited space there would not be a problem. I now understand that Theresa was a breeder that simply wanted a sale. Little did I know the nightmare that loomed before me.

Despite the breeder's abrupt manner it was delightful being surrounded by so many litters. It was also overwhelming trying to decide which kitten to purchase. Theresa became impatient as I must have been taking too long to make my decision. She wanted the sale finalized and her home free of unwanted company. She picked up a little Blue Point Himalayan female I had held earlier and announced, "Well, you seem to like this one." I was uncomfortable as obviously I had worn out my welcome and as far as Theresa was concerned my kitten selection was complete. Although I felt rushed and intimidated by her selling manner I was caught with a bad case of kitten fever and still left a deposit.

Due to the breeder's attitude, I didn't dare contact her until six weeks had passed and my baby was ready to come home. I had wanted to visit my kitten during this period as I'd only seen her the one time when leaving my deposit. However, remembering the breeder's impatience and intimidating manner I was too uncomfortable for any additional confrontation. As a result on the day I arrived to pick up my kitten I barely recognized her. She was only four weeks old when she had been selected for me and now she was a maturing kitten of ten weeks.

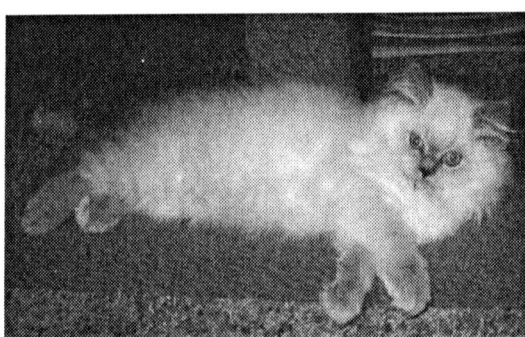

Jennifer: Jasmine's Blue Point Himalayan Female Kitten

After questioning her once again, Theresa reassured me there would be no problems with my two male cats adjusting to the female. With my present knowledge as a breeder I would have provided specific advice to any buyer in that situation. However, in my role as the new buyer I was totally unprepared for the drastic and upsetting changes that soon occurred.

My males were tightly bonded but that relationship

permanently changed when the female kitten was introduced. Theresa should have made my kitten's homecoming easier. However her only interest was money with one less kitten to sell. She had little regard for the well-being of the kitten or the upsetting consequences that took place in my home.

As my contact with breeders increased I soon realized that Theresa's manner was typical of the other catteries in my area. When I started breeding I respected each buyer's unique situation and practiced the skills I'd acquired when in business management. I also recalled Theresa's poor attitude and vowed never to treat prospective buyers in such a manner.

My cattery became a labor of love and is one of my greatest achievements and learning experiences. In my business I used the memory of Theresa's lack of customer relations as an incentive. I've always given my buyers the information and courtesy that I would have appreciated when I was the buyer. In the pages that follow you will have the opportunity to gain from my years of experience and to learn many proven and successful marketing tips.

Testimonials

Here's what other readers have said about Jasmine:

This is what Kelly wrote -

"I received and read your **Proven Marketing Tips for the Successful Cat Breeder** right away. I absolutely love it. You are wonderful and a true blessing. I have only been breeding for a short while and was already discouraged and ready to quit. However, after reading your book I'm ready to improve on my cattery and my cats. Thank you for what you are doing for us breeders."

Nancy's Story -

"I have had an online connection with Jasmine for some time. I have recently acquired a male kitten and brought him into a household with 2 other cats, both full grown.

Enter Jasmine, or the Cat Goddess, as I fondly call her. She has been a wealth of information. She has made many suggestions that we have implemented. Her suggestions have made a great difference. She has a great sense of humor and a knowledge of cats that can only be learned by years of kitty co-habitation. Give her a try and maybe you too will be the lucky Mom of a healthy, happy feline."

Sue writes -

"Thank you so much for helping me solve my cat's annoying night time calling. Who could believe by simply following your instructions I could keep him content and in bed with me where he belongs. I appreciate that you would take the time to help the owner of a domestic cat. I also believe that Jasmine is the 'Cat Guru' of the Internet. Thanks once again!!"

LaDonna's comments -

"I am so excited to find your book. It's just what I've been looking for. I've been contemplating starting a cattery on my own but being employed full-time, on a one person income I could not get answers from the cattery where I bought my precious baby. Thank you! I can hardly wait to get started."

Jasmine's Jewels of Wisdom

The Soul of a Breeder

What essential qualities produce a soul who loves every aspect of living with a multitude of felines?

As a breeder, you are the first person to hold each new life as it enters your cattery. You stroke your queen's swollen belly and remember your own pregnancy. As your queen labors in kittening, you comfort her with soothing words and remember your own long hours of labor.

You bring a book down to your sick stud male's nook to simply sit with him, reading and cuddling for hours. You know there is work to be done however your male needs all your love and attention right now. Somehow everything will eventually be done.

You give up extended vacations and weekends away because no one else knows the routine to keep everyone content within your cattery. Instinctively, you are able to meet every feline's needs so that each precious cat in your care knows they are treasured.

Breeders are unselfish totally dedicated individuals with loving hearts and open minds. Simply taking the time to read **Proven Marketing Tips for the Successful Cat Breeder** separates you from a breeder who only sells kittens.

If the above personality traits match yours then you are on the road to a successful cattery.

A Cattery of Substance

Having a cattery of substance does not necessarily mean having one that is large and affluent. A cattery of substance does not operate on an unlimited budget nor treat its cats as merely breeding stock.

Buyers can always recognize a cattery of substance through the open heart of the breeder. This type of cattery is blessed with an unselfish breeder who is totally dedicated to the fine art of cattery management.

A Breeder of Substance

Breeders of substance respect the special needs of every feline within their care. Time and attention are taken with each buyer to ascertain the perfect feline to blend within the buyer's heart and soul.

A breeder of substance is responsible for each life that is born in the cattery with busy hands for grooming, cleaning stud male nooks and welcoming newcomers into their care.

A breeder of substance is a unique and caring individual. They are quickly recognized as people who have problems meeting their own needs as they are so involved with the many other lives in their care. There is always one more job to complete, one more visitor to view a litter or one more long night of sitting up with a pregnant queen as she is kittening.

Breeders of substance have generous hearts, open minds and are always willing to learn. Thank you for permitting Jasmine to find a place in your never ending day of cattery responsibilities.

Finding a Mentor

Every breeder needs advice and help to create a profitable cattery. However, when do you know that you have found a competent mentor?

A good mentor will want to educate you. A poor mentor will place their needs first by using your success to profit their own cattery. There are many essential secrets that should be passed along from breeder to breeder. Unfortunately, these guarded secrets change from one breeder to the next and even within the different breeds.

That mentor who has become so helpful to you may not have your best interests at heart. If you have found a breeder who is taking on the role of mentor ask yourself the following questions:

1) Do you find yourself questioning your mentor's suggestions?

2) Do you trust your mentor's actions and agree that their methods are ethical?

3) Does your mentor raise the same breed of kitten as you and are you purchasing from their cattery?

4) Do you feel used or taken advantage of by your mentor due to contracts and purchases that appear to work more in their favor?

Proven Marketing Tips for the Successful Cat Breeder
Volume 1 in the Felines by Design Series

1) Do you find yourself questioning your mentor's suggestions?

Always follow your instincts. Although I had an excellent mentor it was his suggestion to purchase three felines sick with ringworm. He found a breeder who was leaving town and the cats she needed to place were worth thousands of dollars. For a few hundred dollars I would be purchasing Top Show Quality breeding felines for a fraction of their original value. The magnificent stud male was proven and the two queens were adult but yet to have their first breeding season. It was a deal too good to let pass by and although I hesitated I felt pressured to follow my mentor's advice. He had gone to a great deal of trouble locating this breeder and I felt obligated due to his kindness.

Within 24 hours of purchasing the cats I discovered that they also displayed a trace of blood within their soft diarrhea formed stool. After a veterinarian consultation, followed by three expensive lab tests, I was further informed that these poor cats were also infected with coccidiosis (coccidia). In addition to treatment for ringworm they would also require additional medication and time to cure this second condition. Coccidiosis is an annoying contagious problem with infected felines carrying the parasite responsible for the condition within their systems. It took months with several additional outbreaks before this problem was properly addressed.

Approximately eight weeks later with a great deal of care my three cats were finally cured of ringworm. However the male suffered through three additional outbreaks as he became known as a "carrier". Such a feline carries the dreaded ringworm infection within their system despite the appearance of being cured. The ringworm infection lies dormant only to reappear. Three years later I was still battling this annoying infection and watching my beloved male depressed by weeks of medication and isolation.

I truly lived to regret my decision. Coming from a family of canine breeders my father had always insisted in only purchasing healthy breeding stock for our family kennel. As a cat breeder I wish to further stress the importance of only purchasing the best quality breeding felines you are able to afford. Ensure that you are conducting business with a reputable breeder and purchase felines with strong compatible bloodlines. You may spend more with your initial purchase but will save many years of breeding and expense to perfect your own bloodline. This holds especially true for your stud male as he is the 'Cornerstone of Your Cattery'. There are few bargains in the Cat Fancy World. As the saying goes, "If it appears to be too good to be true it probably is."

2) Do you trust your mentor's actions and agree that their methods are ethical?

It is best to be of like minds with your mentor. I have known relationships that came to an abrupt end when breeders have tried working together. The same can be said of accepting a mentor's advice in the management of your cattery. If you are uncomfortable with any aspect of your mentor's participation within your breeding program it is best to politely listen but follow your own counsel.

3) Does your mentor raise the same breed of kitten as you and are you purchasing from their cattery?

Unless your mentor resides in an area far removed from your cattery problems often arise when this scenario comes into play. It is unwise to purchase from a cattery too close to your home. It is also unwise to sign any contracts which may limit your use or permit your mentor use of any stud male purchased from your mentor or in partnership with your mentor. Therefore, it may be better to purchase slowly and ask many questions from the cattery where you intend to complete feline purchases.

It is far easier to use cat shows, the internet and web sites such as Jasmine's **Confessions of a Cat Breeder** for unbiased information. If you read or are given the same advice from several unrelated sources and are comfortable with that information chances are it will be right for your cattery.

4) Do you feel used or taken advantage of by your mentor due to contracts and purchases that appear to work more in their favor?

If you are feeling uncomfortable with your mentor then listen but limit your contact with them. Visit their cattery but restrict their access to your own. Do not sign any documents and do not commit to any purchases. When you are in their cattery you will still learn by observing. By not permitting them access to your cattery they will soon lose interest in your breeding program. If you always trust your instincts you will seldom go wrong.

Jasmine had the unfortunate experience of having an unscrupulous, want-to-be mentor interested in her cattery. At one time this breeder attempted to get Jasmine's best stud male into her own breeding program. She did this by sending someone masquerading as a buyer to make an offer. On yet another occasion she asked Jasmine to tell a couple that the Top Show Quality kitten they were buying had died so that she could use him in her own breeding program. Needless to say this breeder never became Jasmine's mentor.

In the following pages you will find the support and

encouragement you need without incurring costly errors and paying the price. You will learn proven methods to attract kitten sales and always maintain your integrity.

Jasmine's Confession of Finding Her Mentor

As with many other breeders I contemplated starting a cattery for several years before I actually began one. Until then in my never ending quest for guidance all I encountered were closed doors. I was hungry for information and a place to begin understanding the complex world of cat breeding.

Attending an annual cat show appeared to be the perfect opportunity to meet breeders and receive the guidance required to start my own breeding program. The large hall was filled with breeders from all over North America proudly showing their beautiful felines. I approached several breeders in an attempt to question them. However their attention was totally focused on the show and they appeared annoyed with my interruptions. Others were overly anxious and willing to promise anything in an attempt to make a sale. I was afraid a breeder would simply sell me any kitten, grab my money and run.

I was intimidated by their breeder jargon and many of the exhibitors did not appear to be interested in responding to my inquiries. My 'buyer beware' instincts were on constant alert while questioning them. I felt terribly shy and was completely out of place totally overwhelmed by the excitement of the cat show environment.

In utter frustration knowing I had accomplished very little I left the show floor. Just prior to exiting the hall I discovered several cat breeding magazines which I quickly purchased. Finally I'd found some information in plain language that I could understand and use to educate myself. After devouring the material in the magazines I began reading the 'Breeder's

Advertisements'. During the next several weeks I wrote to over one hundred catteries in search of information and hopefully some reasonably priced breeding cats.

In my initial contacts I stressed that I was starting and was therefore naïve to cat breeding. However many breeders did not take my situation into consideration. I received many written replies. Some were professionally presented while others were far too informal considering the prices they were requesting for their cats. I was forwarded complex correspondence with detailed cat pedigrees written in endless breeder jargon. The information was confusing and impossible for a novice breeder to interpret.

Today with internet access the situation is far different. If books such as the one you are presently reading had been available to me then I would have saved thousands of dollars. To this end, I have also written Volume 2 in the **Felines by Design** series entitled the **Insider's Guide to Buying Purebred Kittens**. This is an excellent resource for both breeders and buyers. For example, you will discover how to:

- Question the breeder in your initial telephone contact.
- When visiting the cattery know the essential questions many breeders prefer not to answer when you are viewing their litters.
- Know how to present yourself in the cattery without the breeder realizing the extent of your knowledge.
- Be able to identify a correctly priced kitten protected by a sound Ownership Contract.
- Recognize a responsible breeder operating a good cattery.
- Know the correct sequence of questions to ask when speaking with different breeders. As a buyer you will also understand how to interpret the breeder's responses prior to completing your purchase.

Proven Marketing Tips for the Successful Cat Breeder
Volume 1 in the Felines by Design Series

- Know your rights in order to protect your kitten investment.
- Learn the principles of **Kittens by Design** and be able to identify the traits of kittens at various stages of development. It is possible to determine from the many litters you are viewing various personality traits. You will learn to recognize which kitten will eventually become a lap cat, an independent feline or may be the perfect companion for your present cat and will complete your feline family.

This guide is strongly recommended to breeders as they will gain an insight into how they are perceived through the eyes of kitten buyers. With such insights gained sales will increase when breeders incorporate the appropriate changes.

The Insider's Guide would have greatly assisted me with my initial contact with the cattery where I eventually purchased my girls. To have known the right questions to ask in order to receive the answers which breeders are reluctant to disclose would have saved me from wasting money. Likewise, I would have negotiated a better price and realized earlier that I did not receive the breeding quality for the price I eventually paid.

Having been better advised of my rights I should have known to inform the cattery with my dissatisfaction of their assessment of good breeding queens. When purchasing breeding cats sight unseen the buyer must rely on the breeder's discretion and honesty. I purchased my first two breeding queens as kittens from a cattery 3,000 miles from my home. I honestly believe a little disception with a touch of 'cattery blindness' was an explanation for her inability to correctly assess the kittens' quality.

I am now aware that I spent far too much and did not receive the quality which was promised. As an experienced breeder when reviewing pictures of my girls sent from their originating cattery it came as a surprising revelation. With a trained eye, I realized the breeder had carefully chosen pictures which displayed each of the kittens' strongest assets while hiding their obvious faults. Having fallen victim to another breeder's touch of cattery blindness I was determined to be ethical when dealing with other breeders. It became my personal code of ethics to be extremely truthful when selling kittens sight unseen to other catteries. I was overly detailed regarding both the kitten's assets and faults. I would provide in written format exactly why the kitten was priced according to my Cat Association's standard. As a result I never had a breeder question my evaluation of a kitten's quality as I'd been forthcoming from the very first encounter. I felt an obligation to never have one of my buyers repeat my first experience. As a new breeder, I had made a classic error and fell victim to a cattery that had 'kept the best and *sold me* the rest'.

Despite a lesson well learned, this cattery was the only one that made the effort to contact me personally by phone from the one hundred letters I had originally sent. The breeder had been willing to respond at her own expense not knowing if I would ever make a purchase from her cattery. Although the quality of her kittens were questionable, this breeder was willing to educate and offer sound advice despite the distance and money spent on numerous telephone calls. The internet has become a valuable tool for breeders to connect with each other. However the importance of personal contact should not be overlooked when assisting new breeders with their first important purchase.

Although I made several classic mistakes with my first purchases I was blessed with Chantal and Liberty. After travelling by air across the country my four-month-old girls arrived clean and in perfect health. They had been well cared for and obviously loved. So with everything considered at least I'd dealt with a reputable breeder who cared for the well being of her kittens. Not until several months later when purchasing my stud male from the same New York cattery did I realize that all along I had been dealing with two breeders who were working together.

The two breeders where I had purchased my kittens were friends with two separate catteries in different cities. I later discovered that the initial telephone contact was not from the cattery where my girls were born but rather that of the cattery where I was to later purchase my stud male. During the entire transaction I was ignorant of the fact that I had never spoken with my girls' breeder.

When the kittens arrived with their paper work I was surprised to see another name and cattery on the documentation. Although I had dealt with competent breeders I also felt they had taken advantage of my ignorance and should have informed me of this essential information. It seemed unethical that I had never spoken to my girls' breeder and neither felt obligated to share this information with me despite the cost of the female kittens.

When my kittens first arrived breeder gossip spread among the local catteries. Many breeders who had been unwilling to sell open breeding cats to me appeared interested in my newly arrived purchases from New York. Eventually a few local breeders offered my cattery a chance to purchase from their highly prized breeding stock. I soon realized however their ploy was only to have access to my newly purchased 'bloodlines'. In order to make a purchase I was obligated to sign an extremely binding contract. Committing to such a document would have seriously limited my breeding program. To my good fortune, despite the cost and my naïvety, I had actually made a lucrative decision by introducing a new bloodline into the area.

For a while I became accepted as the 'new breeder' and was given some undesired attention. Over time several breeders came to see for themselves my well-known award winning bloodline. Even Theresa, the very first breeder I'd ever met decided to pay my small cattery an unexpected visit. However when she saw my kittens her biting comment was "Are you sure they sent you the right kittens? They just don't look like they belong to their pedigree." She felt I'd made a foolish decision and had spent too much money.

> **If you do not value a person's opinions you should not take their criticisms to heart either.**

Although Theresa's observations were distressing, I decided to follow my own counsel. I have since learned that if you do not value a person's opinions you should not take their criticisms to heart either. The previous year when she realized that I was serious about breeding and would eventually compete with her cattery sales, her only comment was "Don't start breeding, it only brings heartbreak."

My instincts told me she was wrong and the truth remains that despite some heartbreak I encountered more years of joy and made some wonderful friendships with clients that I still cherish today.

I soon realized that the local breeders did not think highly of my breeding program. I was politely advised that most breeders sell out within the first two years. Few catteries appeared concerned that I would last long enough to become any true competition for them. I decided that it was probably better to follow my own intuition, work by myself and remain a 'closed cattery'. Little did I know that six months later everything would change. That's when I was blessed with meeting my mentor.

Bill was a well-known and respected judge with a nationally registered 'Cat Association'. He was internationally renowned and had been a professional cat breeder for many years. I was informed that he had never adopted the practice of providing mentorship to a novice breeder before. It was to my good fortune that for some reason he made an exception for my cattery. I soon realized what an envious position I was in for he was truly a knowledgeable and caring gentleman. Over the course of the next year he unselfishly assisted and guided me with my breeding program.

Bill confirmed that I had purchased two females of only moderate breeding quality. However, genetically they carried excellent bloodlines. He was also well aware of the breeding lines employed by the other catteries within my area. Bill informed me that by shear luck I had created an excellent opportunity for myself. After confiding in him of Theresa's assessment of my girls he appeared amused. Bill knew her well and advised that she never stayed with one breeding program long enough to make it successful. She was always trying to buy her way to success whereas a good cattery uses selective breeding and truly creates their own bloodline. Within my own cattery, he appeared confident that he would be able to arrange stud service from a cat show judge using compatible bloodlines. He knew by using his colleague's exceptional male the results would prove to be outstanding.

After some lengthy negotiations Bill finalized the arrangements and I travelled to his friend's castle of a cattery for the great event. It was only due to his influence that I was granted the use of a Top Show Quality male from what had always been a closed cattery.

Bill had known instinctively that my bloodline would be compatible with this incredible stud male. The resulting litters were the evidence of his vast knowledge. As I embarked on my personal endeavor to perfect my bloodlines and quality of breeding stock I was given information and tips from a professional who was genuinely pleased by the results.

Bill always advised me wisely and due to his expertise I was able to by-pass years of breeding which are usually necessary to perfect a bloodline. With each generation I could see steady improvements which were confirmed by many judges when I travelled long distances to attend various cat shows.

The adventures in my early years as well as my many mistakes and learning experiences could fill volumes. Along with having several want-to-be mentors, I also had experienced breeders trying to convince me to defraud my buyers. Additionally, some breeders in my area tried to purchase breeding cats from my cattery through second parties. Despite everything I truly loved being a breeder.

There are some changes I would have made had I known my mentor earlier. Likewise, there are some suggestions he offered that I might not have followed. New breeders deserve valid information to enable them to become wise consumers. Even with a competent mentor errors are made. It is best to trust your instincts and not worry about offending your mentor. With every decision made your cattery changes. You are the caregiver of your cattery and therefore the final decision should always be your own.

My mentor retired and left the country approximately a year following our meeting. However, in the time we had he gave me a firm foundation and the conviction to believe in myself. I once asked him why he took such an interest in my cattery. Bill paused for a few moments then gave this interesting reply. He said, "I want you to remember me and to use all you've learned to teach others. You have a unique ability for understanding cats. I feel that as a breeder you are truly gifted and will be successful."

As an unbiased mentor through this publication as well as the others available in the **Felines by Design** series[1], I will also pass along many of Bill's tips and words of guidance. I wish to acknowledge Bill and thank him for being such a strong influence in my breeding program. I fondly remember observing him as a judge in cat shows. Bill educated while he was in the show ring and gave valuable information regarding each breed. I never missed a word. I was absolutely mesmerized by his natural ability in handling the most difficult of cats. I especially respected his judging when without prior knowledge he placed one of my own feline entries as his 'Best Cat In Show'.

Wherever you may be my dear mentor please know that I am eternally grateful.

---

[1] Other publications in the **Felines by Design** series are listed on page 85.

How to Advertise Your Cattery

When advertising the less said the better. Buyers are not attracted to a long, fluffy or cutsy ad. A well worded advertisement demonstrates that you are a professional breeder and will bring a better response.

A well presented ad with limited information will attract inquiries from professional breeders as well as the general public. Professional breeders not residing in your selling area are more willing to purchase your Show Quality and hence higher priced kittens.

An advertisement in your local newspaper may be the door to success in the Cat Fancy World. When advertising never provide the prices of your kittens. Buyers may be intimidated by the pricing range and in addition you are providing your competition with information regarding your pricing strategies.

Keep a log of the business calls you receive each time you advertise. If you are permitting several viewings of your litters in one day make notations during your initial telephone conversation. Buyers are flattered if you are able to make reference to any details they expressed in their initial contact. Record the number of contacts, the wording of your advertisement and name of the paper used. You will be able to track the success of each ad if you are advertising at the same time each year. Although I never changed the wording it became evident the number of contacts fluctuated seasonally.

> **It's a proven fact that a professionally worded ad providing limited information will draw a greater number of phone calls and resulting sales.**

The same may be said for stating color types within your litters. Again you are giving your competition the advantage of knowing your breeding program. When advertising incorporate words verifying you are a professional cattery. A buyer is reassured they are dealing with a reputable breeder when your advertisement states you are <u>registered</u>, <u>vet certified</u>, producing <u>purebred</u> <u>vaccinated</u> kittens.

Following is an example of a well worded newspaper advertisement:

> **Registered Persian and Himalayan kittens, vet certified, health guaranteed, (555) 555-1212.**

The less said the better. You also benefit from attracting sales by using fewer words which lower your advertising costs.

Breeders and buyers alike are more likely to call as you have provided only the pertinent information which then becomes an advertising carrot for attracting more sales. It is also advisable to include your area code when posting your advertisement as breeders in other areas of the paper's circulation may be seeking breeding felines. Protecting your valuable bloodline is of the utmost importance. Jasmine only sold 'open breeding felines' outside a 300 mile radius of her cattery. Each breeder will have to decide for herself what the appropriate distance should be.

Never duplicate your bloodline locally.

The following is an example of a well worded advertisement that would be placed in a nationally distributed Cat magazine. You may also wish to include your e-mail address and web site if you have one.

**Blythwoods Purebred Himalayans and Persians:
CFA Registered, Grand Champion Lines,
PKD and Felv negative, Vaccinated, Vet Certified,
Health Guaranteed, Kittens Available,
Adults Occasionally, Closed Cattery, Home Raised
(555) 555-1212.**

Proven Marketing Tips for the Successful Cat Breeder
Volume 1 in the Felines by Design Series

As a professional breeder advertising in national magazines you should consider video taping your cattery indepth. With national exposure you will be contacted by other catteries residing in distant areas unable to personally view your litters. With your cattery ready to view on VHS tapes or DVDs you have greater exposure and improve your chances of selling kittens over a breeder that simply corresponds with e-mails and pictures.

By taping the entire cattery and not just the one litter you are selling, you will be providing a more complete and personal presentation. Your efforts will not only be appreciated by the novice breeder but you may also sell additional cats or kittens from this video exposure.

When a novice breeder is given an indepth profile on tape of your well run cattery it will be shown to many buyers in the breeder's home. You may sell additional cats in this manner to other buyers and breeders who view the presentation. When providing this personal touch and appearing on tape, you become professional advertising for your own cattery.

Your tape will be appreciated by the novice breeder as their own buyers will be able to view the lineage of their bloodline. When a novice breeder experiences a transaction with a breeder of integrity you will become an integral part of that cattery's selling technique. With a professional and personal presentation you are not just training the one breeder but also selling kittens and breeding felines from your own cattery. By receiving greater exposure and implementing additional selling techniques which are to follow, you are more likely to sell your higher priced breeding cats.

The novice breeder and their buyers are willing to pay higher prices for quality kittens and will be comfortable when you are completely open and honest in your cattery presentation. It is best to not provide music in your video as it may be played repetitively. Music may also distract the buyer from fully comprehending your message. Allow the breeder to keep your video. Although some breeders prefer to have such material returned they are unaware that for a small cost they are actually losing future sales. That video may eventually sell kittens for you at another time simply because you permitted the prospective buyer to keep it.

Your video camera, if purchased for this use, all tapes and mailing costs will be a deductible business expense at tax time. Contact your accountant to discuss these and any other possible tax deductions that may be available.

When selling your kittens to buyers your video camera becomes an advertising tool. Take some time to capture on video each buyer's kitten. By recording the litters' growth, litter mates at play and interaction with their mother you are providing your buyer with a wonderful remembrance of their feline as a kitten.

Christmas or the kitten's first birthday is an opportune time to present such a caring gift with a mailed card. I found several of my buyers wanted to repeat the experience of having a new kitten and decided it was time to provide a companion for their grown cat. Your kindness may then be rewarded with another sale. As a breeder I enjoyed interacting with many of my buyers. It gave me a particular joy by re-establishing contact in such an intimate and caring manner. Acts of kindness do not go unnoticed and a caring breeder is one that is remembered by both the buying public and within the veterinarian community.

> **Never underestimate the power of word-of-mouth advertising.**
>
> **Remember that a picture is truly worth a thousand words.**
>
> **Word-of-mouth advertising can be responsible for 50% of repeat sales.**

Promoting Your Cattery

Once many established catteries have sold their last kitten of the season they are anxious to be done with the constant stream of buyers. At certain times of the year the demand for purebred kittens will be steady. Established breeders are proud to say, "Sorry, they are all sold." They tire from the flow of buyers to their home. However, they fail to realize that they are also losing a valuable source of future income when they turn these potential clients away.

After selling your litters resist the temptation to use this standard reply. A far better response is to appear quite open and willing to answer all questions from the potential buyer. Inquire about the type of kitten they are seeking and listen carefully to their needs. I would encourage the buyer to view the litters that were sold. If the kittens have already gone to their new homes provide the buyer with a video of your cattery with the promise of additional litters in the near future.

Many of my litters were sold with deposits left for a specific coloring and sex of kitten by viewing present litters or those on video. When a buyer is exposed to the different color types your cattery is able to provide, your video library becomes a wonderful selling asset.

I found some breeding combinations would continuously throw Show Quality kittens which were then sold for professional showing and breeding. Other combinations would provide kittens with incredible personalities. I had a long list of buyers waiting for a kitten from a particular breeding pair due to the loving and engaging personalities of their litters.

I always reassured the buyer that their deposit was refundable at any time. However, due to the reputation of my cattery my buyers seemed content to wait for the next breeding season. I also knew which stud males and queens to breed to provide the combinations of kittens that were already sold. As a breeder, with time you will come to know your breeding pairs extremely well.

Potential buyers will enjoy seeing the cattery and visiting the mother of the promised litter. If you provide clients with your time now you will not have to re-advertise when the pregnant queen's litter is ready to be sold. Your kittens will already be sold while other breeders will be just starting their advertising during the next breeding season. As such you will be ahead of the advertising market.

> **In this manner you will usually find that your kittens are pre-sold from last year's advertising budget.**
>
> **During the Spring breeding season other breeders will be just starting to advertise the many kittens available in your area.**

I would always tell my clients that they may leave deposits for the next available litter. They would also be informed that each queen was only bred once every ten months. Although it would take time to provide a specific sex and color point kitten many buyers were willing to wait and were comfortable leaving a deposit. Their deposit would be refunded should the intended buyer's circumstances change or they simply decided not to purchase. When a buyer is given such flexibility they will leave a deposit as you will be recognized as a professional and ethical breeder.

When the queens' litters were delivered I would inform all my buyers that the great event had occurred. Each buyer knew that the kittens would be viewed in the order that the deposits had been received. Kittens were usually seen at four weeks of age with buyers selecting their kitten during the first viewing. Although a buyer was never pressured into making a quick decision they knew that they were viewing a pre-sold litter. They were aware the next buyer's right to view could possibly select their kitten of choice. Buyers appreciated the option of holding a place for a special kitten of choice and knew the sooner a deposit was left the greater the selection of kittens they would have when the litters were born.

Every time you have a potential buyer visit your cattery it is a professional courtesy to extend a business card. Business cards are retained when they are both informative and attractive. If you make your business card into a fridge magnet it will be worth its weight in gold and serve as a constant reminder of your cattery. If you have a litter picture of your kittens on the magnet it will be admired repeatedly with your name being passed on as well.

You can create your own professional looking fridge magnets at home with a computer and a deskjet printer using Microsoft Word or any other program of your choosing. Simply purchase the blank magnets at any stationery or department store and create an attractive and professional design on your own computer. By creating your own designs you not only save money but you can also update or change the designs at any time to suit your needs.

Cat shows are very popular. Everyone from breeders to the general public will be collecting business cards. It is best to have at least several hundred inexpensive cards with you. Many people go from one cage to the next taking a card from each breeder. As large cat shows are crowded it may be difficult for a potential buyer to find you without a card showing your cattery name. I also had t-shirts made which displayed my cattery name on the front and back. Anyone associated with my cattery in attendance at the show wore these t-shirts. This enabled buyers to more easily locate me.

While seated with your cats in the hall or busy grooming in preparation to enter the show ring people will gather around to watch. Never limit the number of cards available as often you may be showing a cat in one of the rings and be unable to answer questions.

Likewise, it is also a good idea to provide brochures that potential buyers can keep and review at home. Clearly identify your cattery's name, breed, your name, telephone number, web site, e-mail address, Cat Association, etc. on the cover. The interior can detail the history of your cattery and your particular breed. These brochures can easily be prepared and updated using Microsoft Powerpoint or any other software program on your home computer and printer. An 8.5"x11" sheet of paper can be used to print these brochures and simply folded into three parts. Some spectators are looking for kittens and use the opportunity of attending a cat show as there are many breeders available.

Despite the work involved when showing, a potential buyer will be more willing to visit your cattery if you show respect and take time to answer their inquiries. This also presents the opportunity to view other breeders and their manner with potential buyers. I soon realized there was more socializing between breeders than an interest in assisting potential buyers.

> **When attending cat shows, have the least expensive cards available with the most important information provided.**

When a serious buyer is present and anxious for information provide a quality business card. Then make an appointment for them to view your cattery. Displaying the name of your consulting veterinarian on your cards, with their permission, demonstrates that you have nothing to hide with respect to the health of your cattery.

> **Vets are a valuable source of information as well as referrals.**
>
> **Some buyers will only accept a vet's referral.**

Promoting Yourself

During your initial contact with a buyer by phone it is of the utmost importance to demonstrate patience, kindness and your continued availability. Jasmine would reassure a buyer that she would always be available to them for any question or problem during the lifetime of their cat. We guarantee that few buyers ever received such consideration from other catteries when purchasing a kitten.

Do not be uncomfortable by giving this reassurance to the buyer. As your level of knowledge increases along with your cattery profits your contact with previous buyers will be limited. It was my experience that only 10% of buyers needed my advice. However I welcomed their contact as each problem became a learning experience for me.

Take comfort in the knowledge that as an intelligent and well informed breeder you always have access to your mentor, your vet, as well as many other sources of helpful information including our web site. Questions may be posted on Jasmine's Feline Message Forum.

www.confessionsofacatbreeder.com

> **Jasmine is also available for online consultations with <u>reduced fees</u> for breeders who have purchased any of her publications.**

When speaking to a potential buyer by phone or in your cattery it is more beneficial to educate. Do not follow the fearful practice of other breeders by limiting your wealth of information. Instead, inform your clients that you recognize their right to ascertain the health and integrity of each cattery they contact including yours.

As a breeder who is honestly concerned with the success of the buyer the selling of an individual kitten becomes unimportant. Breeders with integrity are remembered and the cattery name is passed on to other potential buyers.

At times breeders find themselves playing matchmaker between a buyer and kitten. Some buyers appreciate a breeder's interest in their lifestyle when attempting to select the perfect kitten. Such attention demonstrates sincerity that the breeder is not totally focused on only 'making a sale' but is also concerned with the mutual compatibility between the buyer and kitten.

> **Keep the cattery welcoming to the buyer even by phone. Provide as much information as they appear willing to learn.**
>
> **If you are open and willing to educate you will be the exception to the rule. You will be remembered and your name will be passed on.**
>
> **Every call is important!**

Some Essential Questions for Breeders

Inform the buyer that they should ask each breeder they contact the following set of questions:

1) How long has the breeder been in business?

2) What age does the breeder allow the kittens to leave the cattery?

3) Are there any cats in the house that are permitted outside access?

4) Does the breeder take in other cats for breeding purposes, ie. Is it a closed cattery?

5) Is it a caged cattery or are the kittens 'home raised'?

6) Are there any genetic faults in the cattery?

7) Are the cats and kittens vet checked and vaccinated on a regular basis in the vet's office?

8) Is the deposit refundable if financial circumstances change or if the buyer changes their mind?

9) How long does the breeder guarantee the health of their kittens?

The above are only some of the essential questions that buyers should pose to breeders. Explanations for the purpose of requesting this information follows:

1) How long has the breeder been in business?

With each situation whether the buyer encounters a novice or an established breeder there are advantages and disadvantages to be considered.

Advantages of New Breeders:

1) A new breeder is anxious to please and eager to sell her kittens. She is more willing to advise her buyers of the various kitten personalities in her litters. If a breeder has spent time with her kittens she will have a better idea of their distinct personalities and should advise the buyer accordingly.

2) A new breeder may price her kittens lower than an established cattery. A registered kitten should be priced

according to how closely they meet the breeding standard in the cattery's registered Cat Association. A new breeder may have one price for all the kittens due to her inexperience interpreting the Cat Association's standard. The novice breeder may also price her kittens lower due to a lack of confidence or knowledge of the current market price for her breed. If a buyer is not interested in showing but wants a purebred loving pet this may be an ideal situation.

3) New breeders show a greater interest in handling their babies. The benefits of being raised in a loving family atmosphere are numerous. Kittens adapt more readily to their new home. They also tend to be more social and ready to bond with their new owner. With continual handling a new breeder will develop a more affectionate nature in her babies.

4) When a kitten is handled from birth the breeder develops an affection for her kittens which greatly assists the babies to later bond with their new owners. The breeder will be able to provide detailed information regarding the personality of each kitten and assist the buyer with their choice of the perfect baby for them. When a kitten is handled right from birth they learn how to show love and affection. Some babies are responsive to their breeders even prior to their eyes opening around the tenth day. Kittens soon learn that no one can replace Mom but they enjoy the warmth found in their breeder's hands and will readily respond to a warm soothing voice.

The earlier the contact with their breeder the better. A few moments several times a day benefits both nursing Mom and babies. When the breeder takes time from her cattery schedule to give affection to litters and nursing queens everyone benefits. The Mom is reassured her owner is nearby and the isolation of caring for kittens never becomes overwhelming. Some queens become fearful and when overwhelmed tend to move their litters several times a day for protection when they are kept in isolation. The breeder benefits with affection from her queens during the litter stage and their relationship intensifies after the kittens are gone. Tight bonds develop when a breeder takes time to give additional care to her litter mothers.

5) The handling of newborns assists in sales as the kittens enjoy being held and are more personable with their potential owner. Kittens that have not been handled appear skittish, aloof and distant. The implications of a more affectionate kitten will assist the buyer to finalize the transaction whereas a kitten displaying feral tendencies will be the last to sell.

6) A new breeder is far more likely to permit a buyer weekly visits to enable the buyer and kitten to bond.

Disadvantages of New Breeders:

1) A new breeder is learning and may not be as organized as an established breeder. She may not accurately time her buyers' visits properly or may have buyers arrive on her doorstep just as her kittens are ready for a rest.

2) Problems may occur with registration papers. There is much to learn when registering litters and a new breeder must maintain accurate records when dealing with her Cat Association. She may not advise her buyers that they must return with their vet's 'Certificate of Castration' before individual kitten registration papers are issued.

3) She may not protect her kittens' breeding rights or the buyers' purchase rights by signing a 'Kitten Contract' also known as an 'Ownership Agreement' that protects both the

cattery and buyer.

4) She may incorrectly sex her babies. In other words at birth she may incorrectly identify males as females and vice versa.

5) The new breeder may accidentally prepare the wrong kitten for their homecoming day if the litter had identically colored kittens. In one instance where all the kittens had identical coloring I have personally prepared the wrong kitten for their homecoming day. I learned to then color tag my kittens and that situation never occurred again.

6) Some new breeders become overwhelmed after their first couple of litters and simply stop breeding. This can be devastating for a buyer should a problem occur and the new breeder does not feel obligated to provide compensation for the kitten.

Advantages of Established Breeders:

1) An established responsible and registered breeder is worth their weight in gold. If a cattery has been in operation for at least four years and has maintained a sound relationship with the same veterinarian they will be strongly recommended.

2) If the buyer ascertains that a cattery is a labor of love and the breeder is welcoming and willing to discuss all issues of feline ownership, the kittens will sell quickly. To find such a breeder is well worth the risk of leaving a deposit and waiting for a healthy kitten from parents with a strong genetic background.

3) When a cattery has been in operation for a while the buyer is able to view the schedule and the breeder will have a good idea of what her breeding pairs are able to produce.

4) A breeder should not be offended if a buyer requests to view the pedigree of a litter. She should be willing to explain a kitten's heritage and also show interest in the new home where her kitten will be living. Some established breeders will actually visit the new home before and several weeks after her baby has joined the new family. The buyer should not take offence in the breeder's interest but rather understand the breeder cares about the kitten and would be available should problems arise as the kitten ages.

5) Litter registration and individual kitten registrations with Cat Associations should be maintained by a responsible breeder. Once the kitten contract has been satisified with the feline's altering the breeder will readily assist the buyer in registering their kitten.

6) An established breeder that is willing to permit viewing of her breeding cats usually does not have a problem within her cattery that she is fearful to have exposed.

Disadvantages of Established Breeders:

1) Breeders with cattery issues are fearful to expose additional visual information to buyers as they may lose potential sales. The established breeder may not permit a buyer to view her stud males or the living quarters of her breeding females or nursing queens. Often seasoned breeders are seriously reluctant to permit any access to their breeding stock even to buyers that have just purchased a kitten. They simply want to make their sale and have the buyer leave.

2) A breeder that does not permit cattery viewing may be worried that the buyer will see cramped and dirty quarters for caged kittens and breeding males. If a cattery is not kept clean

the scent of a spraying male will be strongly evident. When breeding males are simply used for stud service they may either distance themselves or become extremely agitated when their breeder is nearby. Lack of affection for stud males promotes shorter life spans. A stud male should also be given an opportunity to explore outside their cage on a daily basis. After serving their purpose in the cattery's breeding program a caring breeder will locate an appropriate home and pet out her stud male. This can be safely accomplished if the stud male is altered. Not every male continues to spray and mark their territory after they have been altered. A stud male can be extremely affectionate and deserves the opportunity to become a beloved pet.

2) What age does the breeder allow the kittens to leave the cattery?

The purpose behind requesting this information will determine whether the cattery is more concerned with profits or the welfare of their kittens. It is a crime for a breeder to release her kittens prior to 10 weeks of age. Depending on the circumstances nine weeks is an acceptable age if the kitten is not left alone during the day.

The first five weeks of a kitten's emotional development are beneficial for bonding with Mom. During the following five weeks the kitten's life is dedicated to social development gained through playful interaction with litter mates. Motor skills are perfected through play and also exploring the breeder's home. Kittens that are unfortunately restricted to a caged existence are severely limited in their social development. They learn to only trust Mom and the kittens with whom they interact. Depending on the size of the cage the kitten may develop timid feral behavior or become overly agressive due to living in caged small quarters.

If a breeder is reluctant to release her babies early she is more concerned with the kitten's health and emotional development than her profits. Kittens are not only time consuming work but there is also the combined cost of food and litter expenses which accumulate during this period of time.

When purchasing a kitten where an air flight is necessary the baby should not be transported until it is at least four months of age. Be wary if through a lack of interest in the kitten's welfare or simple ignorance a breeder is willing to ship any earlier.

3) Are there any cats in the house that are permitted outside access?

Be an aware consumer. If a buyer is made aware of domestic pet felines having outdoor access the cattery is providing an unsafe environment in which to make a purchase. This is a recipe for disaster as any outside cat exposes the entire cattery to a wide range of fatal feline diseases. The breeder will also be coping with the inconvenience of flea infestation, ringworm and ticks. Prior to their first series of vaccinations kittens have developing immune systems and are highly susceptible to infestation and disease. Many breeders simply ignore the problem which is then inherited by the new owner.

Attention should also be given to outside exposed cages for breeding cats. If the breeder has guarded her cages from migrating felines the cattery is able to function safely and stud cats are provided with the best of both worlds.

4) Does the breeder take in other cats for breeding purposes, ie. Is it a closed cattery?

Should a breeder suggest the availability of one day breeding a kitten you are viewing with one of her stud males it is best to purchase elsewhere. Often breeders are unable to ascertain thevalue of a developing kitten's possible breeding potential to their own cattery. By petting out and selling a breeding quality kitten the breeder receives immediate payment and is not committed to the expense of the kitten's care. They are then given the opportunity to assess the kitten fully grown with the buyer assuming the cost and care of the future litter. Your feline will be exposed to any infection within the cattery during the breeding process as will the felines within the breeder's care. A breeder that adopts this practice may be increasing their profits however the risk of disease within her cattery becomes a serious issue. It is best to use your time in this cattery as a learning experience only.

While a responsible breeder, employing strict standards, may offer stud service to select preferred breeders they lose the benefits of being a closed cattery. A closed cattery offers buyers the reassurance that all litters have been raised in a healthy environment and have not been exposed to disease.

5) Is it a caged cattery or are the kittens 'home raised'?

Large catteries concerned with caring for multiple litters have been known to cage their kittens from conception to leaving the cattery for their new home. Such a breeder is able to maximize the space dedicated to her breeding cats and raise a larger number of kittens. Caged cats are simply far easier to care for with the mothers rarely permitted a rest break from their babies. Only the breeder's pocket book benefits from such an arrangement as this is not a healthy environment for either queens or kittens.

If you are presented with a large cattery of caged kittens take the opportunity to note the differences of play and interaction between caged babies and home raised kittens. As indicated earlier, a caged kitten's personality will be altered and there may be a delay in coping with the larger space provided within the owner's home. Freedom from caged life may result in a kitten becoming skittish or indifferent to bonding with their new owner.

6) Are there any genetic faults in the cattery?

The importance of requesting this information lies in the truthful response of the breeder. Every breeder encounters some problems. It is best to purchase elsewhere if the breeder becomes defensive or is too adamant with a negative reply. Only a cattery in the infancy stages of it's development can be believed to state a negative kitten mortality rate in it's genetic history.

Only a responsible breeder will show comfort responding honestly to this extremely important question. Every cattery will have a few kittens during it's breeding program that may inherit genetic problems. Congenital heart defects are not uncommon and although may be inherited are usually discovered prior to the kitten's departure from the cattery. PKD, Polycystic Kidney Disease, is one that may not surface until the kitten is grown.

Unfortunately not every breeder would consider refunding the cost of a grown cat due to this condition. It is important that the buyer request this information and have the breeder's written guarantee that there is no record of PKD in their kitten's genetic history. It is absolutely imperative as a new breeder when purchasing breeding cats to have this guarantee. As you are purchasing the foundation for your cattery you will be responsible for any PKD kittens sold even if you were unaware of the pre-existing condition in your own breeding stock.

7) Are the cats and kittens vet checked and vaccinated on a regular basis in the vet's office?

Breeders are always trying to save money and increase their profits. However trips to the vet or diet for the kittens are not areas that should be scaled down. It is best to ask the breeder if she physically takes the kittens to her veterinarian for their first vaccination series. Some breeders self-vaccinate with live serum which they purchase directly from the manufacturer. Other breeders will have a veterinarian come right into the cattery. Neither is an ideal situation.

Vet's coming directly to the cattery may use the opportunity to mass vaccinate litters without each kitten receiving a thorough examination. With breeders vaccinating or vet's using the opportunity to mass vaccinate issues such as heart defects are sadly missed. A kitten with a congenital problem may pass through the cattery and become a heartbreaking loss for the new owner.

8) Is the deposit refundable if financial circumstances change or if the buyer changes their mind?

When a buyer has this reassurance they are comfortable leaving a deposit. Such flexibility indicates to the buyer that the breeder is reasonable and that they are more likely to experience a trouble free transaction. Such a breeder will receive word-of-mouth advertising which may result in 50% of repeat sales.

9) How long does the breeder guarantee the health of their kittens?

A breeder should guarantee their kitten's health in writing for a period of 48 to 72 hours after leaving the cattery for any contagious diseases. Once a kitten has left the protective closed environment of the cattery they are subject to disease from other felines in the buyer's new home. It is believed any contagious disease the kitten contracts after a 48 to 72 hour period is due to the care of the new owner. It is best to have your kitten vet checked within that time frame which may also be the opportune time for the 2nd series of vaccinations. The vet may also be able to detect other problems which should be reported to the breeder when examined within the 48 to 72 hour grace period. A vet will verify the kitten was purchased in ill health and the responsibility will then be upon the breeder. When a kitten is examined shortly after leaving the cattery and found to be in ill health by a veterinarian it will then become a legal matter if the breeder refuses to issue a refund.

It was my policy that should a feline die before their first birthday a kitten was offered without charge from my next litter. Depending on the preference of the owner if a new kitten was not welcomed I would also refund the original purchase price of their baby. My vet did not believe this was my responsibility. However, it met with my business code of ethics and was appreciated by my buyers. Unfortunately not every breeder feels the necessity to extend such a kindness. Although first year mortality circumstances are rare such a cattery will be well respected within the veterinarian community and their kindness will be remembered by the buyer.

Many other essential questions are explored further in Volume 2 of the **Felines by Design** series.

> **By educating your buyers you are informing them that you are an ethical breeder who can be trusted and are more likely to make a sale.**

Buyers assume you are an open and honest breeder when educating them about the many problems that can occur in other catteries. They will seldom purchase elsewhere as they do not want to take chances when they have already found your cattery to be a perfect one for them. It becomes a combination of fear to explore the unknown and the safety of a compassionate breeder with a clean cattery. Why would they want to look anywhere else?

Helpful Cat Show Hints

It is wise to not leave your cats unattended during cat shows while socializing with other breeders. If you are unavailable for questions then provide photo albums of your cattery, kittens, stud males and queens. People love pictures and kittens sell themselves.

While showing a cat in the ring it remains a good policy to always have someone seated with your other show cat entries. This will not only ensure your feline's safety but any interested buyer will be reassured of your return to answer their enquiries.

Many breeders look bored sending off 'leave me alone' messages that a potential buyer will recognize. As a result buyers will walk away as will their check books. Cat shows are long and tiring with breeders listening for their competition rings to be called. Nevertheless even seasoned breeders should be willing to assist a potential buyer. A breeder should always present themselves with a positive attitude and welcoming persona.

> **Future litters will also be sold if you attend cat shows on a regular basis.**

As Jasmine Says...

I once attended a local cat show simply as an observer. As with many breeders I was in my element and the atmosphere was like an aphrodisiac. I enjoy speaking with other breeders especially when they are unaware that I am a seasoned breeder and feline behavior consultant. It is also intriguing to share information with breeders and to observe their various selling techniques with the public.

My purpose in attending the show was to purchase an American Shorthair kitten for a friend. For the next hour I questioned many breeders especially those with kittens to sell. In general, they appeared reluctant to provide information and were not very helpful. This was a new breed for me, and naturally, I was inquisitive about their nature, cost, etc. Had any of the breeders been more open and forthcoming I may have made a purchase. I was particularly unimpressed by one breeder's policy to not provide any health guarantee at all following a kitten's purchase.

Walking away from the caged area, I was greeted by a client who had purchased a kitten from me several years ago. She was accompanied by a friend who was interested in buying a kitten and they immediately began questioning me. Within several minutes a small crowd gathered to listen. After a short time I was surrounded by an increasing number of buyers asking questions as if I was lecturing for the cat show.

As the group increased in size I became uncomfortable as the Managers of the show were obviously watching me. I realized though that my experience was not unique. There were other potential buyers experiencing the same lack of interest as I had with the American Shorthair breeders. The public was interested in purchasing kittens but unfortunately the breeders appeared more concerned with the show than their sales.

There is so much information to learn as a buyer. Many seasoned breeders become complacent and fail to realize that each buyer's knowledge and situation is unique. If you enjoy interacting with the public you will be the breeder that attracts more inquiries and hence more interest in your cattery. Many good breeders are too concerned with the cat show and have no idea how many buyers they are neglecting or future sales they are missing.

Successful and Proven Selling Techniques

Kittens are cute and basically sell themselves. The cutest stage for selling your litters is at four weeks of age. The kitten has not yet developed the motor skills for exploring and enjoys the simple pleasures of being cuddled and playing with their litter mates. Kittens at this stage of development enjoy being held and interacting with potential buyers. If you are careful with timing your appointments according to the litter's schedule a buyer experiences the pleasure of all aspects of bonding with the right kitten.

It's wise to inform the buyer that at this early stage of a kitten's development they should not expect the same level of affection during their next visit. Every week the kitten will enter a more advanced stage of development and may not welcome as much personal interaction until they leave the cattery. If the new owner is not provided with this information you may possibly receive a phone call following their next visit and you will have lost the sale. Furthermore, having been advised of this stage during a kitten's development, your buyer will be more inclined to trust any additional information you may offer in the future.

Although some buyers do enjoy listening to stories about the parents of their chosen kitten, others would prefer to not be bored by your latest cat show conquest. Also a breeder only complicates a sale by using breeder jargon. Some breeders practice various forms of lecturing or provide undesired detailed information that may not be welcomed. Buyers are excited when purchasing a new kitten and may not always show interest in the dynamics of running a cattery. The longer you breed and sell your kittens the more quickly you will recognize the different selling techniques needed for various buying styles. When you are able to adapt your selling presentation to match the individual buyer's needs your kittens will be sold more quickly.

> **A good breeder will recognize the difference between the buyer who wants to learn about the cattery and the one who makes their decision by playing with and silently observing the kittens.**

It is far better to be a listener in this type of situation as listening completes sales. Excessive talking will bore your prospective buyer right out the door.

> **It is more important to meet the buyer's needs than to have the buyer meet yours.**

Your self-esteem should not become a part of your breeding program. Your concern should always be centered on your kittens and the people who want to buy them.

The first viewing of your kittens should be five days after the introduction of solid foods to their diet. Changing from mother's milk to solid food may result in diarrhea and the buyer may be concerned that the kittens are in poor health. It is also best not to feed your kittens just prior to a viewing. With a full stomach, most kittens become lethargic and just want to sleep. With practice you will be able to judge your litters' schedules and stagger appointments during their play times.

A good time for viewing is after nap time and between litter play times. During this period kittens are more conducive to cuddling and will bond more readily with their potential owner. Your buyer will have the enjoyment of first watching the litter at play and once play has settled down a baby will welcome being handled.

Although males are often just as affectionate as females many buyers prefer one sex over the other. Some buyers are also determined to have a certain color. It is wise to stress that personality is the most important consideration for bonding with a cat. You can advise a buyer that once the cat has been altered, they would be left with the personality rather than the sex.

In Jasmine's cattery her Himalayans were usually sold prior to her Persians. Before a buyer viewed the litters, the most popular kittens that were already sold and hence no longer available were removed. If the buyer decided that they did not want one of the Persians in the viewing area, Jasmine would then present a sold Himalayan Seal Point. She would reassure the buyer that this color point kitten would once again be available within a few months. The buyer was then given the option to reserve a kitten and would leave a refundable deposit. Thus the cattery did not lose a sale.

In every cattery there is often a 'feline star'. The feline star loves to perform and will usually be the official greeter as each new buyer comes to the cattery. In Jasmine's home Caterina was the star. She loved to escort everyone who came to view the litters. She enjoyed the role of meeting each prospective buyer at the door and enticed them to then follow her to the kittens.

Due to her loving intervention many buyers simply wanted another Caterina. She was a Seal Point Himalayan and there was never a Seal Point kitten left after Caterina wove her magic spell.

Caterina

Kitten fever is a condition described as an uncontrollable urge to have a kitten at any price. Good sense flies out the window with the buyer following their heart regardless of their personal circumstances. Used car dealers know the look of a first time buyer and often take advantage of the situation. A good breeder proceeds with caution using kindness and does not exploit the buyer's vulnerability.

Allow the buyer to view the litter. However request that they delay making a decision and not leave a deposit until the following day. If you accept a deposit from a buyer with signs of kitten fever a refund may be quickly requested when they realize their error in judgement.

By accepting a deposit under these circumstances a kitten is considered sold. However, by showing consideration for the kitten fever victim and not immediately accepting a deposit your kitten is still available. Your next appointment may be an aware consumer who has researched the breed and knows exactly the type of kitten they wish to purchase. By using sound business practices and not taking advantage of a kitten fever victim you have not lost the sale. It is beneficial with many kitten fever victims to simply confirm another appointment to return within a few days. By displaying such consideration your potential client has the opportunity to consider their decision before committing to purchase.

Pictures, Pictures, Pictures!

When your litter is four weeks of age, take your first formal litter picture. In this instance it is best that the babies not be at play. Several litter pictures at various ages from new born to 8 weeks may be provided with other assorted gifts when the kitten leaves the cattery.

I believe what distinguished my cattery from the others in my area were the small cattery gifts I provided on the day the kitten was leaving. Some of my clients were so touched they became overwhelmed by a few small gifts. It was truly a delightful experience which I enjoyed. I provided each kitten with a little furry toy mouse which were abundant in the cattery. Kittens first learned how to growl when these favorite mice were introduced to them around four weeks of age. The furry mice would rattle when shaken as the kittens held it in their mouths. I believe the popularity of this toy was the rattling which immitated the shaking of a dead animal and was a primeval connection for the kitten. The furry mice were held captive and litter mates were always challenged to a battle during play time. Providing such a toy during viewing would entertain buyers and gave great insight into the distinct personalities of each kitten.

I would also provide a sample of their diet including both wet and dry food. Samples were provided at a nominal charge by the pet food distributor where I purchased all my supplies. As a smart businessman the owner provided discount coupons which I included with my kitten gift packs. These coupons allowed the new kitten owner to receive a discount off their first purchase of food or other supplies. I was the only registered cattery he would recommend when questioned where to purchase the specific felines I was breeding. Much to my surprise he never mentioned it himself. However I received feedback from my buyers advising me of his referrals when I would provide them with the discount coupons.

I purchased a small supply of cardboard feline carrying cages which I kept on hand for buyers who did not realize the necessity of transporting their kitten. Often such buyers had purchased a proper cat carrier but left it behind in their excitement of bringing their new baby home. It was not an expensive investment but whenever I assisted the buyer with a new temporary kitten carrier they were extremely grateful. It cost very little for the cattery to leave a lasting impression of thoughtfulness.

A copy of **Cat Fancy** or **Cats Magazine** was also provided depending on the number of copies I was able to obtain. I preferred to give a copy showing the month of the kitten's birth as it was more meaningful to the new owner. Despite the popularity of these two wonderful magazines many of my buyers had never experienced the pleasure of discovering either magazine.

When attending cat shows I also accumulated various samples of toys, food, litter and various other free gifts supplied by companies promoting their merchandise. Inexpensive cat toys and gifts can also be purchased in wholesale lots from eBay, dollar stores and any number of other liquidation outlets. I was never at a shortage for products to add to my 'Kitty Gift Packs' which changed depending upon the availability of items.

I took the time to provide a typed letter detailing information regarding the kitten's mother and father. The new owners were also totally delighted with the additional details of their kitten's personal growth and development. I also included a picture of the litter and one with the kitten's favorite litter mate at play. Upon receiving an invitation to visit my kitten's new home I later discovered that many times both pictures were framed and on display. Sometimes it's the most simple acts of kindness that touch the buyer's heart. I soon realized my greatest reward was simply being appreciated and respected as a breeder.

A kitten at four weeks is at their most engaging age. A good marketing strategy is to have saved additional pictures of each kitten in the litter at this same age. You can enclose an individual photograph in a Christmas card to the owner of the kitten at the right time. This becomes a non intrusive but personal greeting that will touch the buyer's heart. Buyers will also view your gift as confirmation of your original commitment to maintain contact with them.

Spring is not far away and seeing their cat as a baby may prompt a call for another kitten. You may also honor the first birthday of their baby by sending a cattery birthday card including pictures of their kitten at play with litter mates.

The Compassionate Breeder

Breeders often receive telephone inquiries from buyers who are grieving the loss of a beloved feline. It has become imperative for them to only purchase a kitten of a certain color or sex. As a compassionate breeder it is best to suggest that they may require time to come to terms with their recent loss. An ethical breeder does not capitalize on a buyer's grief.

Permit the caller to visit your cattery and play with your available kittens without any additional pressure to purchase. Your thoughtfulness will be greatly appreciated and they will realize that you respect their loss.

Jasmine advised such clients that it was unwise to choose a kitten solely based on color or sex in an effort to mimic the look of their deceased feline. Every kitten possesses their own distinct personality and selling a kitten where expectations and personality have already been decided will eventually disappoint the buyer. Chances are with such sales the kitten's true personality will never be permitted to fully develop and the baby will be returned.

> **The message here is to be known as a breeder who cares.**

You may encounter some buyers viewing a litter of kittens who enjoy reminiscing about cats from their past. Kittens may be sold simply by listening compassionately and sharing with the buyers' loss.

Jasmine has witnessed a buyer under these circumstances immediately bond with a kitten while holding her and speaking of a long lost feline. While the buyer shares their personal experiences of a beloved lost cat a spiritual connection would pass between the buyer and kitten. Although there are no words to explain this interaction a sensitive breeder will learn to recognize the signs of such a connection. It becomes a breeder's special privilege to witness this intimate bonding with a buyer and one of their kittens. Once you have shared such an intimate experience you will have gained a greater insight which other breeders would envy but never quite understand.

Breeding Schedule

When a breeding program is in effect, you will have your litters spaced to eliminate kittening problems with queens. A good practice is to have compatible pregnant queens ready to deliver within a few days of each other. A mother-daughter or sister-sister combination usually works well. Additionally, in Jasmine's cattery there was always one 'baby sitter'. A female who couldn't carry her own kittens but would nurse and care for every kitten who needed her.

Much depends upon the size of your cattery and breeding program. Jasmine realized with experience that it was best to space a total of six litters during each breeding period. She would have two litters still nursing and immobile. The second set would be her four week old kittens now ready for viewing while the older kittens at ten weeks were leaving the cattery on a staggered basis.

For the mothers of the kittens now leaving it was comforting to have the younger babies emerging from the nursery. Jasmine soon realized this timing was beneficial to both sets of mothers. The newer mothers were given a chance to recover from the constant responsibility and care of the young litters. These young kittens now provided an ideal distraction for the mothers of the mature departing litters. With the absence of the sold kittens the mothers were offered the opportunity to nurse if they so wished. When given access to nuture the four week old babies the more maternal queens did not experience as difficult an adjustment as their mature litters left.

This combination worked well and provided a substantial income during the entire breeding period. By adapting such a rotation schedule the queens were never overbred. Depending on your breeding program you are then given the opportunity to continue the same cycle using your next set of breeding and pregnant queens^2.

> **Inform your buyer that you only breed queens at ten month intervals and thus have fewer litters available at one time. In so doing you are demonstrating a love for your cats that they will not see in other breeders.**

With the additional income from deposits for future litters your cattery will have a continuous income while other breeders are struggling to survive. When a cattery is always open to new buyers there are few slow periods as kittens are usually sold well in advance.

> **Having more kittens may generate immediate income however a good reputation generates respect with profits.**

---

^{2} More breeding info. is provided in Vol. 4 of the **Felines by Design** series.

Jasmine's List of Absolute Do's and Don'ts

Absolute Do's

- Present yourself as the cat loving person you truly are. As a breeder you enjoy the process of living with breeding cats, caring for stud males and welcoming new babies into your cattery. A breeder that loves her cats has an obvious enthusiasm visible to anyone viewing her kittens. Such an affection for your feline family cannot be forced or reproduced for the benefit of buyers in your home. This isn't a complicated process, simply be yourself.

  When you are comfortable with the buyer don't hesitate to show affection for your cats. There are buyers who appreciate a breeder sharing her feline idiosyncrasies. Others will prefer you remain silent and allow them to speak of their own experiences. Some buyers are more comfortable with a breeder who will permit them to make their choice by quietly playing with the kittens. These buyers simply select their kitten after a short period of time. They place a deposit then quickly leave. The longer you deal with the public, the quicker your expertise will help you decide which role to follow for each sale.

  🐾

- Show integrity in your business dealings. Integrity cannot be bought or found anywhere as it truly must come from the breeder's heart. Integrity is a priceless commodity that will have your buyers return again and again because you have earned their respect and trust.

An ethical breeder will never switch kittens after a sale or change prices according to how wealthy the buyer appears. An honest breeder will refund the price of a kitten if genetic faults appear within the first year and the baby dies. A breeder with integrity does not believe the price of a kitten should fluctuate according to the local competition or seasonal time of year.

A responsible breeder not only loves her kittens but also enjoys dealing with the public. Although profits are important for a caring breeder there is satisfaction that her kittens have been placed within safe and loving homes. There are many fine catteries with good business practices and such breeders thrive.

- Listen when the buyer speaks. Much can be learned of a buyer's true needs by listening carefully to everything they say. This is a level of respect which the buyer may not have received in other catteries.

By listening you will develop the skill to recognize similar personality traits in your buyer which may be reflected in one of your kittens. For example a quiet person may understand and appreciate the qualities present in an affectionate but gentle female. Your rambunctious 'leader of the pack' male would be more at home in a social and outgoing family where other felines may be present.

The principles of **Kittens by Design** are discussed in Volume 2 of our **Felines by Design** series. You will learn how to recognize the different personalities of kittens at the various stages of their development and which buyer will provide the best match. By following the principles of **Kittens by Design** your kittens will flourish when placed with the right family. Such felines reach their greatest potential and grow to become cherished members within their families. You may even be responsible for finding someone's treasured feline soul mate.

The longer you breed and listen to the public the better skilled you will become when acting as a matchmaker. There is always a compatible feline ready to love and bond with the ideal client. With experience your skill will develop and there will be a growing list of buyers waiting for your call when their 'special' kitten has been born.

Approximately four 'special' babies were born each year in Jasmine's cattery. These lovable kittens were full of personality and Jasmine instinctively knew which family on her waiting 'wish list' was right for the developing personality. Jasmine's clients were confident and trusted her to select the right kitten for their family even if it took time. The sooner these kittens were promised the easier it was for Jasmine, as a breeder, to separate her heart from her desire to keep 'just one more kitten'. This situation became even more difficult when a favorite kitten was almost good enough to keep for breeding.

- Do speak when the buyer needs information. Although it does help to love breeding and socializing with other cat lovers, you may find the routine of selling kittens to be very repetitive. Nevertheless try not to give the impression that you are irritated with answering the same repetitive inquiries.

A sensitive buyer may be uncomfortable when repeating questions and it is therefore your responsibility to put them at ease. Remember at one time you also asked the same questions when you were learning. Such consideration displays your true nature as a breeder with respect and compassion.

- Always be positive as negativity loses sales. A positive attitude attracts sales.

Having positive energy is more than just being pleasant to buyers. When you love your work it will be reflected in your communication by telephone and within your cattery while you are showing your kittens.

- Make sure the cattery is not only sanitary but maintains a clean scent.

Book appointments after a general disinfecting and cat grooming. Offensive odors may lose a sale. However other people are equally offended by the heavy scent of concentrated cleaning products.

Some breeders will burn incense while others provide a continual fragrant potpourri simmering in the environment. Small, electric potpourri pots placed in strategic areas will add a pleasant fragrance within your cattery home during viewing hours. It is best to check the water level in your potpourri pots between viewings and to ensure that they are unplugged after the last buyer has left the cattery.

It never fails that when a visitor arrives some cats due to excitement will feel the urge to use their litter box. When such a natural event occurs inform your buyer that its true interpretation is a sign of respect. This feline is welcoming you into her home.

Still More Absolute Do's

- Once the buyer has made a kitten selection take them with their baby to your private office or a quiet room away from interruptions.

By leaving the kitten play area the buyer will have the opportunity to finalize their decision and not be distracted by the other litters at play. You will look more professional and the buyer will have an opportunity for further bonding with their chosen kitten.

Your office is an ideal location for buyers to sign contracts and view your collection of ribbons and rosettes from attended cat shows. You may also wish to display litter pictures and posters of your personal cattery stars. It is relatively inexpensive to have posters made from your favorite cat photos to decorate your office.

Buyers will maintain a sense of security when they are able to personally observe your certification. You should frame and hang documentation from the National Cat Associations where you are registered. The more professional your office presentation the more secure your sale will be.

- After making their kitten selection and leaving a deposit for their chosen kitten, it is crucial that you invite the buyer to visit their baby often. Kittens grow quickly and ideally many buyers should return once a week.

These weekly visits will be comforting to the buyer who will enjoy witnessing the rapid development of their new kitten. It is beneficial for the kitten as they will continue to bond with their owner. Also when leaving the cattery the kitten will more easily adjust to their new home.

Having provided such flexibility for your clients they will remain confident that you have not withheld any information regarding the health of your cattery or kittens. When you are generous with your time you will be respected as a considerate breeder. It will become evident not only with your clients but within the veterinarian community that your cattery is truly a labor of love.

By implementing the above techniques the new owner and their kitten will have an opportunity to develop a stronger bond. Breeders maintaining such high standards rarely have their kittens returned. Once comfortable with a cattery a buyer not only recommends the breeder but often returns for a second kitten. It may be additional work to have buyers visiting every week but the advantages are far greater.

Jasmine had one buyer who each week brought either a friend or family member to visit her baby. The kitten had been only four weeks old at the time of purchase. During the next five weekly visits, three of the buyer's family also bought kittens from the same litter or placed a deposit on the next litter.

- Sometimes it pays to be generous with your time.

Although it was not Jasmine's intention, she made some valuable lifetime friendships. Cat lovers are basically loyal and affectionate people. Just sharing a love of cats with some buyers will develop into a lasting friendship.

Each satisfied buyer will become an enthusiastic ambassador of your unique welcoming persona. Every kitten you sell will generate additional sales for ultimately it is the buyer who will speak highly of your reputation and integrity within the breeding community.

- Many buyers will elect to use your personal veterinarian.

You have most likely attained your vet's respect having used their services to vaccinate and treat your cattery on a regular basis. As your cattery becomes successful and the vet's clientele increases your cattery may be eligible for additional privileges.

Your vet has been exposed to and heard of many cattery horror stories from within the closed veterinarian community. After viewing your cattery in operation and receiving positive feedback from your many buyers you may be recommended as his 'breeder of choice'. Veterinarians are also pleased to welcome kittens back into their practice and meet your buyers. His respect for you will also increase as it is upon your faith in his practice that he has been chosen as a veterinarian for your buyers. Vets appreciate a recommendation by a thoughtful caring breeder that they also respect. Your vet is aware of your cattery's health and will realize that you have a special ability to attract kitten sales which in turn increases his own practice.

Once you have attained your vet's confidence word may be passed around your city and state that you are a 'good' cattery. This information will also be shared within the veterinarian community as good breeders are difficult to find. Once your vet realizes that your business ethics are strong he will recommend your cattery within his practice. Eventually, other practices within the larger veterinarian community will also be comfortable recommending their clients.

- Try to involve your family in the daily cattery routine.

You will need a break and many small tasks shared will give each member of your family a sense of self esteem as the cattery flourishes.

- Keep all cattery receipts and engage a trusted accountant who will guide you with submitting any tax deductible business expenses.

A large check at income tax time could provide a family holiday.

Absolute Don'ts

- There are situations where dealing with the public will become challenging. As a professional breeder you must never allow your personal feelings to become evident to the buyer.

It can become irritating when a buyer's indecision over their choice of kitten becomes overly time consuming. Rather than displaying impatience it is far better to gently assist in their choice of kitten. Much depends on a buyer's lifestyle and living conditions.

As a responsible breeder you are aware of the various personalities within your litters. Question the buyer to ascertain their personal preferences for a kitten. This will assist the buyer to focus on their individual situation and you will have an opportunity to show kittens that are more likely to blend comfortably within their household. These principles of

Kittens by Design are discussed in Volume 2 of our **Felines by Design** series.

- Never neglect the cattery dental care for each and every member within your breeding program.

Your felines deserve good oral hygiene care as provided by your veterinarian. Each of your breeding felines should be vet checked for dental care with the procedure spaced throughout the cattery according to need. With each litter of kittens sold one of your breeding cats should be checked for this procedure.

When your kittens are vaccinated the mother of the litter can easily be brought with her babies to your veterinarian. With time each of your stud males and queens will eventually be vet checked for good oral care. When this procedure is spaced throughout several breeding seasons your good reputation will once again be passed throughout the medical community. A breeder that provides this necessary but often ignored medical aspect of breeding will be respected by veterinarians. That in itself is worth its weight in gold.

Although dental care is a vitally important procedure it is often neglected by seasoned breeders. Fearing a loss in cattery profits many fail to realize their breeding stock is truly their most valuable asset. The expense of proper dental care spaced throughout an extended period becomes a considerable tax deduction. However, most importantly it may ultimately increase the life expectancy of their treasured and expensive breeding cats.

- Do not refer to your stud male's quarters as a cage. Use the word 'nook' and make it as spacious and comfortable as possible.

Try to improve your male's boredom by supplying love and interest to his life. A stud male does not have to live to simply reproduce. Jasmine loved her stud males and was equally loved in return. If you provide your males with special attention they will not only love and appreciate you but your breeding program will also improve. Males are easier to handle and they will enjoy servicing your queens when they remain content within their environment.

- Do not show impatience with a buyer.

When necessary excuse yourself and leave the room. Should a buyer show inconsideration and overstay their welcome or speaks inappropriately take your frustration elsewhere. If you are alone during such a situation de-stress by leaving the viewing area to vent your anxiety. Take a few moments to jot several lines on your computer or in a journal. Contacting a friend by telephone for a short private chat works wonders when dealing with a difficult buyer.

Should a buyer remain longer than necessary never give the impression that their business is not wanted. It is best to excuse yourself. Contact a neighbor by telephone and ask them to make an appearance. Buyers seldom stay when the next scheduled appointment arrives.

Never hesitate in following your instincts whether it involves your cattery's health or your own personal safety. If at first sight you are uncomfortable with a situation inform the person right on your door step that the kittens have all been sold. It is imperative that you do not permit them entry to your home. Although most breeders are able to judge the sincerity of buyers from the first telephone contact it is always possible to misjudge a situation.

Whenever possible ensure that a family member is nearby. If you want a buyer to leave immediately every family member should be aware of a coded emergency phrase. Once that phrase has been used it will alert them that you require assistance. A trusted outside contact should also be notified that if you telephone them and use the same phrase they are to come to your assistance immediately.

As you develop and trust your breeder's instincts you will seldom go wrong.

Conclusion

Confessions of a Cat Breeder was formed to assist novice breeders and buyers seeking purebred kittens. Our goal is to assist new breeders so that they may start successful catteries and prevent costly errors when establishing their breeding program. We also want to help buyers identify catteries with ethical breeders selling healthy registered kittens.

It is hoped that you have found the preceeding pages to be informative with tips that will assist you within your breeding program. In conclusion Jasmine would like to leave you with a story from a breeder that she encountered that demonstrates the value of reading this book.

Bonnie's Story

I have a nightmare story. I spent $4,000 on 4 British Shorthairs from a breeder who lived on a multi-million dollar estate in Vermont. She also bred Maine Coons, and Norwegians. This woman is now in New Hampshire, and she is still running her cat mill business where the inbreeding is preposterous.

I am an experienced breeder of Scottish Terriers with people on waiting lists for my dogs because I was so selective in my breeding practices. I wanted to start breeding cats and thought I was going into this with my eyes open. Bottom line, many innocent, harmless kittens died due to congenital defects resulting from inbreeding. I wish I could make this known to a lot of people. I have one cat left and he is a magnificent big male named "Tom". This facility was perfect in every way and I was duped.

Jasmine's Response

I sympathize with you as unfortunately I have heard this story too many times. It is my goal to assist both breeders and buyers from falling victim to similar circumstances. I advise people to study pedigrees to ensure line breeding was conducted selectively. I also adhered to selective breeding practices within my own cattery. Despite waiting lists for my kittens I preferred to safely breed my queens every ten months. Fortunately I have never encountered a congenital defect due to line breeding in my own cattery. However, I am aware of catteries where this is a regular occurance due to breeders not respecting genetic boundaries necessary to maintain a healthy bloodline.

In my work as a feline behavior consultant and cattery mentor I assist breeders to ensure this situation does not occur. I advise all breeders to carefully interview the cattery where they intend to buy. A large cattery is not necessarily the best place to spend your hard earned dollars.

Someone who is breeding too many unrelated breeds is likely overwhelmed with work and consumed with making money. Producing numerous kittens and providing stud service can be profitable. However, it also ignores the well-being of cats and kittens.

Should you contact a breeder with more that two litters of kittens of the same age at the same time, you may have encountered a kitten mill situation. A responsible breeder, in a smaller cattery, should have no more than two litters immobile and nursing, two litters of small toddlers, and two litters that are sold and ready to leave the cattery at any one time. A breeder cannot properly take care of her kittens unless the size of the cattery is limited. Smaller catteries may be less prosperous but in the long run they are more productive.

When purchasing a kitten, whether Breeding or Pet Quality,

it is important to request the name of the breeder's veterinarian. When dealing with a responsible breeder the cattery's health records should be revealed to the purchaser upon request. Should the cattery be reluctant to supply this information then take your money elsewhere.

Bonnie I sincerely hope that you can put this experience behind you. Should you need any guidance in establishing a breeding program **Confessions of a Cat Breeder** will be pleased to assist you.

Publications & Services from Jasmine Kinnear

Felines by Design Series

Volume 2: Insider's Guide to Buying Purebred Kittens
Volume 3: Insider's Guide to Selecting Domestic Felines
Volume 4: Insider's Guide to Starting & Managing a Cattery

Additional volumes in this series will be forthcoming.

A Companion to the Felines by Design Series

How to Hide Your Cat From the Landlord:
A practical approach to assisting everyone
in the pursuit of owning a feline

Services

Request your very own **personalized consultation** with Jasmine. **Confessions of a Cat Breeder** is presently offering the following services to help you with your kitty's needs:

- Breeder Consultations
- Behavior Consultations
- Cat Owner Consultations

For more information visit our web site:
www.confessionsofacatbreeder.com

How to Contact Jasmine Kinnear

Should you have any questions regarding this publication, feline behavior issues, managing or marketing your cattery we welcome your inquiries on Jasmine Kinnear's **Confessions of a Cat Breeder** web site. Please sign the Guest Book then explore our Feline Message Forum, breeding tips and feline stories. We further welcome our readers who wish to share their own personal experiences with their favorite feline.

www.confessionsofacatbreeder.com

Glossary of Breeder Jargon

The following definitions will greatly assist a buyer to communicate on a breeder's level when purchasing a kitten. Also, for the new breeder appearing knowledgeable and informed will prove to be a valuable asset when purchasing breeding stock or attending cat shows. Finally, it can only assist the experienced breeder to review the following terms to further strengthen their communication skills when conversing with fellow breeders and potential buyers alike.

Altered: Breeders use this term to describe a feline that is unable to reproduce due to the surgical removal of the male or female reproductive organs. Veterinarians describe this procedure as 'castration'. The term 'neutered' for a male and 'spayed' for a female is also used to describe this procedure. The slang term 'fixed' is also used by the general public and applies to both sexes.

Breeders and purebred cat owners with altered felines compete under the classification of 'Alters' in the major Cat Associations. During the last two decades the standard of 'Alters' has risen sharply. It has become a highly competitive classification with Breeders presenting 'Top Show Quality' cats that were once breeding in their cattery.

Competition under this classification is no longer open to someone who just wishes to show their beloved purebred. It is now necessary to purchase a higher priced 'Show Quality' kitten with a right to show clause stated within the 'Ownership Agreement'. If you wish to show your altered purebred you will first have to obtain the breeder's permission prior to show entry acceptance.

Breeders are usually pleased when their cattery name is given Cat Show exposure without incurring any additional advertising costs. If you intend to show, ask the breeder to take this into consideration when pricing your chosen kitten. If you agree to display the cattery business cards at each show you may pay a little less for your kitten initially.

Backyard Breeder: This term is used to describe non-registered breeders. Although they may sell their kittens at reduced prices, their litters are not necessarily purebred. Backyard breeders have usually broken contracts when purchasing their cats and do not own their cats' 'breeding rights'.

Bloodline: Breeders commonly use this expression when speaking of their cat's genetic background. Each breeder is looking for the perfect bloodline to compliment the 'cattery look' which they are attempting to achieve. The elite and most prestigious catteries will sell their breeding stock to new and established breeders for a considerable sum of money. The purchased cat will be reproducing using the name from their birth cattery as a bloodline. The new breeder may prefer to use the best known cattery on the purchased cat's pedigree as their bloodline of choice when advertising litters from that bloodline.
   Also see **Cornerstone of Cattery** and **Campaigning a Cat**.

Breeder Quality: Breeding Quality females with strong genetic bloodlines are highly prized within a cattery. Although physically not the best show examples of their breed they are valued genetically. When bred to a male with compatible bloodlines these queens are able to produce both Show and Top Show Quality kittens. Kittens displaying the Breeder Quality standard are often sold to responsible breeders attempting to raise the standard of kittens within their cattery.

Breeding Program: Good breeders will have a program in place where it has been decided which of their cats will be used in the next breeding season. It is the desire of every good breeder, with the careful blending of bloodlines, to perfect the standard of their breed and obtain a 'Best of the Best' in every attended cat show.

Breeding Rights: In order to breed a cat, you must have an agreement with the cattery to obtain full breeding rights with the purchase price. If the breeder insists that you sign a contract restricting your breeding male or female, you must protect your rights. This glossary can assist you in understanding complicated breeder jargon in contract form.
Also see **Open Cat** and **Cattery Blindness**.

Breeding Yourself Into a Corner: This occurs when an established breeder is unable to safely continue reproducing kittens genetically from the breeding stock they are using. When this situation occurs the breeder must seek a new bloodline to keep the cattery safe from genetic faults.
Also see **Line Breeding, Out Cross Breeding** and **Twice In-Once Out**.

Campaigning a Cat: Some breeders will spend thousands of dollars travelling to attend cat shows in the United States, Canada and when highly successful will proceed by showing in worldwide competitions. Should a cattery produce a 'Top Show Quality' cat, a breeder must decide whether to take the financial risk of travelling week after week competing in numerous shows. When a cat continues to do well in competition, the value of the cat and the resulting litters from that cat's bloodline are financially promising. The more shows attended, the higher the cat may be placed in the Association's 'Top Show Cats of the Year'.

Although the breeder will spend a great deal of her tax deductible income the cat may ultimately provide a lucrative income for the entire cattery. After a year of campaigning, the breeder may stud out her prize male for a very high fee or sell his kittens worldwide to other breeders who desire to duplicate her success.

Also see **Throws Better than Himself** and **Cornerstone of the Cattery**.

Cat Association: The Cat Fanciers Association (CFA), The International Cat Association (TICA), and the American Cat Fancier's Association (ACFA), to name just a few, are the professional Cat Associations known worldwide. These organizations register catteries and purebred litters. In order to be a 'registered breeder', a cattery name must be accepted by a chosen Association. Each individual cat's bloodline must be proven by registered pedigree if not already registered within the chosen Association.

Each Association monitors the results from professional judging within their registered cat shows. Every breeder anxiously watches the mail at year end to be notified where their campaigned feline star will show in the Association's 'Year Book'.

To learn more you may visit each association's respective web site below:

The Cat Fanciers Association (CFA)
    www.cfainc.org

The International Cat Association (TICA)
    www.tica.org

American Cat Fancier's Association (ACFA):
www.acfacats.com

Catlet: This is an affectionate term for a kitten that is in the awkward stage of not yet being a fully grown cat. A catlet is still growing by leaps and bounds but has left the adorable baby stage. It is extremely important that nutritionally a catlet should still be considered a kitten. Not quite a kitten but too young and small to be referred to as a cat. The typical catlet is usually full of energy and always getting into trouble.

Cattery: A cattery is the place where cats are bred and the resulting litters are born. Some catteries may become quite large with the cats residing in a separate building on the breeder's property. In many cases, the larger catteries cage their stud males, queens and litters to make the handling of so many cats and kittens easier. Some kittens live their first few months with little human contact. This may result in a fearful kitten when it is finally released into the buyer's new home.

Many breeders prefer to keep their catteries to a moderate size and provide a home raised environment. The 'stud male' will have to be caged. However 'queens' and litters will have the freedom of the home and be handled by the family on a daily basis. It is far easier for a kitten to make the transition into a buyer's home if raised lovingly in the breeder's residence.

Cattery Blindness: Cattery blindness is simply an inability to see the faults in a kitten from your own cattery. Most breeders will admit to the occasional lapse of judgement when pricing a kitten.

Some breeders do not accept criticism well. A kitten's value becomes the breeder's interpretation of how closely it meets their Association's standard of breed. As a breeder in continual contact with her own bloodline, she becomes accustomed to the look of her own breeding. Sometimes a breeder will make errors in judgement when selling a kitten to another breeder.

Jasmine almost became a victim herself when she considered keeping a kitten for breeding. After questioning a friend for her opinion of the feline the faults were pointed out with her selection. She admitted that her friend's observations were correct. Additionally, Jasmine also maintains that she has shown kittens in cat shows that were judged by the very breeder of her stud male. A judge often prefers their own bloodline which is only enhanced after another breeder has spent additional years duplicating and improving it. In that particular show Jasmine received 'Best Kitten' in that judge's ring with varying placements from the other judges in the same show.

Also see **Pet Quality**, **Breeder Quality**, **Show Quality** and **Top Show Quality**.

Cattery Look:

It becomes evident when attending cat shows that even within the same breed, each cattery uses different bloodlines to establish their own look. If you are interested in a particular breed of cat, it is preferable to attend shows to become familiar with the look of the breed that you are considering buying.

Certificate of Castration:

When a feline has been altered the veterinarian will issue a signed Certificate Of Castration. This document is to be presented to the cattery as evidence that the owner has honored the buyer's agreement to have their cat altered. Once spayed/neutered the breeder should present the individual kitten application to the owner to register their feline. The breeder has registered the original litter with their Cat Association however the individual kittens remain unregistered.

The kitten owner must decide on a registered name for their cat and submit payment with the completed form to the breeder's Cat Association. Many buyers are unaware that their cat is not registered unless they complete this important last procedure.

Chirping, Vocalizing: Purebred and domestic felines both male and female love to 'chirp' and communicate by using different pitches of vocalizations with their owners. Should you own a feline that enjoys vocalizing it becomes one of the most intimate acts you can share with them.

There is an entire vocabulary behind your feline's attempt to communicate with you. It can be a wonderful challenge to identify your cat's speech patterns. If you are blessed with such a cat, listen then share the conversation by responding. Your cat will enjoy your human attempts to communicate on their level and the bond between you will become even stronger.

Closed Cattery: The safest catteries are closed catteries. The breeder will not accept queens in for stud service despite the added income this practice can generate. A closed cattery will not board cats, not even kittens they have sold in the past which is again another source of additional revenue. Closed catteries do not keep a pet cat that is permitted outside access. This situation has put entire catteries out of business after having to destroy all their cats and litters due to a virus brought in by the resident outside domestic.

When a closed cattery purchases breeding stock some breeders follow a standard practice of a short isolation period. If the new cat appears healthy within a limited period of time the new member is introduced into the general cattery population. This is not the best method for introducing new felines into a closed cattery. The entire procedure of buying and selling purebred felines using proper cattery management is discussed in Volume 4 of the **Felines by Design** series.

Cornerstone of the Cattery: Professional breeders fondly refer to the stud male as the cornerstone of their cattery. Stud males are usually the cattery's most expensive investment and can make or break the breeder's good intentions. Despite a cattery's budget when it comes to this feline cost is only a part of the equation. A stud male's pedigree must be researched extensively with consideration given to the bloodline's compatibility currently used within the cattery.

Some breeders will purchase a 'Breeding Quality' female in an endeavor to avoid the expense of buying a 'Top Show Quality' male. The breeder is attempting to produce her own male through a paid stud service to avoid the high cost of purchasing a proven stud male. There are simply too many risk factors involved including jeopardizing the health of the queen. It becomes a genetic and financial gamble to hope a stud service is going to duplicate a Top Show Quality male in one litter of kittens.

Cremation: Cremation is a private matter that is rarely discussed until a loss occurs and a decision must be made. Many pet lovers feel that the separation of burial is too final so cremation becomes an important issue.

Before surrendering your pet please note that crematoriums, unless instructed otherwise will cremate many cats and dogs simultaneously. Each owner is then given an urn of accumulated ashes. If you wish to receive only your own cat's ashes it is essential that you request a 'private' cremation. Although a little more costly for many feline lovers in bereavement it is the only option.

Many animal hospitals will charge an additional service fee

for handling these stressful details when such a loss occurs. However if you have a family friend who is able to deal directly with the crematorium and provide the transportation of your beloved pet, there will be less expense.

I have spoken to many feline lovers who have requested that their own ashes be scattered with their beloved cat's ashes. I made the same request several years ago when the idea was presented to me by my six-year-old son Mark. For some reason the thought is comforting and as I correspond with other cat lovers I realize I'm not the first to have such a wish.

Daft Half Hour: This is the burst of excess adrenaline and hormones, particularly in breeding cats, which begins a long run, chase and play of two or more felines. Jasmine has witnessed this phenomenon many times in the cattery. It can be triggered by one rambunctious feline and creates a chain reaction for the other members of the cattery.

Jasmine's cattery had several poles, one over 14 feet high. Her cats would chase each other in a mad dash up and down, like running an obstacle course, until all participants were exhausted. All human occupants, non-participating felines and kittens kept a clear path until the chase was over and cattery normality was restored.

Jasmine claims that this activity was a joy to behold and everyone took pleasure in watching the cats run their cattery circuit for about 30 minutes -- hence, the name daft half hour. The balance of the day was consumed by their other favorite pastime otherwise known as rest. A cattery fact... night is for sleeping, day is for resting.

Domestic Cat: It is always disturbing when some owners refer to their beloved pets as 'just' a domestic. Domestic cats appear to have longer life spans than many purebreds and are just as beloved to their families.

A domestic cat is more often than not the result of a backyard breeding encounter. Domestics are fortunate to not be as restricted by a limited gene pool as are many purebred felines. Provided a domestic is offered a good diet and resides in a loving inside environment they can bless their owners by living a long and healthy life. When the sire of a domestic litter is a 'feral cat' his kittens may inherit his wild nature.

Fading Kitten Syndrome: This condition is similar to Sudden Infant Death Syndrome (SIDS) in humans, also known as crib death. It is an unexpected and sudden death in kittens. For my own emotional health I refused to bond with a new litter of kittens until the danger of Fading Kitten Syndrome had passed.

The litter may be born and appear healthy with all kittens nursing normally. A fading kitten may appear within 24 hours to as long as 9 days following the birth. The symptoms include a loss of interest in nursing with the litter mates increasing in size while the fading kitten remains small. Within a short period of time the baby loses body heat, is unable to digest bottle feeding and quickly dies. Liberty, my best mother, always knew from birth when a fading kitten was present. She would quickly end its misery by lying on the baby to hasten death.

A breeder should carefully observe the mother with her kittens. When this condition is present, many queens know instinctively the signs that will eventually alert the breeder. Deaths resulting from fading kitten usually occur within the first 72 hours. The longest surviving fading kitten in my cattery succumbed on the ninth day.

On the 14th day, once the kittens' eyes have opened the occurrence of fading kitten is less likely. Although breeders handle their kittens several times a day it is best to remain professionally detached until this time. Once the eyes have opened it is not difficult to bond and permit yourself the luxury of loving your babies. The mother of the kittens will appreciate your affection while the litter will continue to thrive on the personal interaction.

It must be understood that not all kittens displaying the signs of fading kitten are victims of Fading Kitten Syndrome. There are also circumstances when a veterinarian should be consulted. I now have a male cat that displayed every sign of having this fatal condition. However, he became the exception to the rule as he readily accepted bottle feeding and was able to digest KMR formula. Presently 10 years old my Tally Ho loves to sleep on my lap while I work on the computer and holds the official position of office cat.

Felines by Design: A breeder that has spent time with her kittens is able to successfully match kittens with the right buyer. A **Kitten by Design** shares similar characteristics as the owner. When a perfect match occurs a **Kitten by Design** develops into a **Feline by Design**. Owners will proclaim an amazing lifetime blending of souls with their cat. In future sales many buyers will only accept a feline if it has been proclaimed by the breeder as the perfect **Kitten by Design** selected just for them. Only a **Feline by Design** can truly become their owner's Feline Soul Mate as they are eternally bonded.

Feral Cat: A true feral cat is one born in the wild with little or no human contact. The feral cat has a shortened lifespan and usually lives and breeds in the wild totally independent of human care.

Keep the Best and Sell the Rest: This term is used to describe breeders who are known to keep the best kittens for themselves and sell the rest to novice breeders. While it is understandable that an established cattery must always be improving their own breeding program it is terribly wrong to deceive and overcharge a novice breeder.

As a naïve breeder, Jasmine fell victim to this practice with her initial purchase. She paid for 'Show Quality' breeding females but instead received two moderate 'Breeding Quality' females. Nevertheless, she was able to produce 'Top Show Quality' kittens within her first five years of breeding. Read **Jasmine's Confession of Finding Her Mentor** on page 23 to find out how.

Kitten Contract: This document is also known as an 'Ownership Agreement'. When purchasing a purebred feline buyers are informed that the cattery maintains ownership of the feline's breeding rights. When purchasing a kitten the buyer does not maintain any rights to breed their cat. Only the cattery has breeding rights to kittens born within their cattery. Once purchased as a 'pet' the breeder may still own the breeding rights but the purchaser legally owns their feline. A contract is signed in agreement to have the cat altered at the appropriate age. The contract should also stipulate further conditions to protect the kitten such as the buyer will never declaw their cat, will not permit the cat outside access and will provide annual vet checks and vaccinations as required. Contracts vary according to the breeder and the buyer should be careful before signing any documentation if not in agreement with the terms.

Kitten Mill: A kitten mill occurs when someone is over breeding and has a large number of kittens for sale. All felines including kittens are caged and the cattery may have other unrelated breeds also available for sale. Although the breeder may be registered she is likely overwhelmed with work and consumed with making money. Producing numerous kittens and providing stud service may be profitable however it ignores the well-being of cats and kittens.

Should you contact a breeder with multiple cages of kittens for sale you have probably encountered a kitten mill situation. A responsible breeder in a smaller cattery will have a limited number of kittens available. There should be no more than two litters immobile and nursing, two litters of small toddlers, and two litters that are sold and ready to leave the cattery at any one time. A breeder cannot properly take care of her kittens unless the size of the cattery is limited. Smaller catteries may be less prosperous but in the long run they have fewer health issues and are more productive.

Kitten Birth Certificate: Often a backyard breeder attempting to project an aura of authenticity will generate an official looking certificate of birth on their computer. Such an *unofficial* document may be referred to as a Kitten Birth Certificate.

When purchasing from a breeder such a document may be an indication that you are not viewing a registered purebred litter. Even if the terminology 'sire' (stud male) and 'dam' (queen) are shown on the certificate this is now a case of buyer beware. Kittens purchased from this litter will never receive registered documentation from a Cat Association. Although the parents of the kittens may be registered cats the owner has not purchased and does not own the breeding rights. The litter cannot be registered nor will the buyer ever be in a position to later register their purchased kitten. Without proof of registration a buyer may not be purchasing a kitten from a registered purebred litter.

A 'backyard breeder' may also use a Kitten Birth Certificate in an attempt to charge more for their litters. Jasmine is aware of innocent buyers who received this document when they unknowingly paid the same price as a fully 'registered kitten'.

Also see **Stud Male** and **Queen**.

Kitten Fever: This condition is known as an uncontrollable urge to have a kitten from any breeder at any price. Good sense flies out the window and the buyer follows their heart with little regard for their personal financial circumstances. Used car dealers know the look of a first time buyer and may take advantage of the situation. However a good breeder proceeds with kindness and caution without exploiting the buyer's vulnerability.

Kittening: A 'queen' in labor is known to be in the process of kittening.

Kittens by Design: A breeder that has spent time with her kittens is able to successfully match kittens with the right buyer. A **Kitten by Design** shares similar characteristics as the owner. When a perfect match occurs a **Kitten by Design** develops into a **Feline by Design**. Owners will proclaim an amazing lifetime blending of souls with their cat. In future sales many buyers will only accept a feline if it has been proclaimed by the breeder as the perfect **Kitten by Design** selected just for them. Only a **Feline by Design** can truly become their owner's Feline Soul Mate as they are eternally bonded.

Line Breeding: Many catteries from time to time will incorporate the practice of line breeding. When a breeder employs this procedure she is attempting to intensify the strongest assets within her bloodline.

When an 'out cross breeding' produces a Top Show Quality female that displays the best qualities of her breed this practice is often used. As the sire and dam were bred from unrelated bloodlines the daughter is then bred back to her father. If the breeder retains a second female kitten from the resulting litter she will be unable to breed the stud male in future breedings using that immediate bloodline.

Some breeders prefer to breed the original Top Show Quality out cross kitten to a second out cross male. Should this union produce a promising female kitten that kitten would be finally bred to the original stud male, her Grandfather.

These are two classic examples of line breeding. It is believed the highest quality standard of a breed may be produced by adopting this method. Although this procedure may take a breeder many years to incorporate, the kittens produced are often outstanding representatives of their breed.

The above is an abbreviated explanation of a very complex genetic breeding practice. Greater detail and thorough explanations in simple to understand language of how to accomplish these breeding techniques are explained in Volume 4 of the **Felines by Design** series.

Multi-cat Household: The true feline lover always has room for one more cat. Jasmine believes that although problems occur while personalities adjust to one another, every cat should have a compatible feline companion. When three cats or more are residing in your home, you are truly blessed with belonging to a multi-cat household.

Non-registered Purebred: Backyard breeders produce non-registered purebred kittens. Although the parents are registered, they were purchased as pets only. The 'backyard breeder' has broken a contract to alter their male or female cat. The parents are registered but the cattery of origin has not released the cats' breeding rights.

Protect your investment by learning how to identify the backyard breeder. Many backyard breeders will produce computer generated documentation that may confuse the buyer into believing they have purchased a 'registered kitten'. A kitten should not be considered a purebred without possessing the legal Cat Association documents as proof. Without registration papers the pedigree is not guaranteed to be true.

Open or Open Breeding Felines: Any purebred feline that has not been altered is referred to as an open feline.
   Also see **Whole Cat**.

Out Cross Breeding: When catteries have been operating for several years breeders may find themselves with genetic difficulties and have created a situation referred to as 'breeding yourself into a corner'. A healthy solution is to have an appropriate 'out cross breeding'. Although costly, it is a method that may perfect and improve the cattery bloodline.
   A stud male is bred to a female with neither cat sharing any genetic bloodline history. It is the breeder's decision whether to purchase a cat for this purpose or to obtain stud service. Many breeders are pleased with the quality of litters produced when the right 'out cross breeding' pairs have been used. It truly becomes a matter of good fortune as even extremely good quality 'out cross' pairs may result in little more than an entire litter of 'Pet Quality' kittens.
   The above is an abbreviated explanation of a very complex genetic breeding practice. Greater detail and thorough explanations in simple to understand language of how to accomplish these breeding techniques are explained in Volume 4 of the **Felines by Design** series.

Overbreeding: This occurs when a female is bred each time she comes into heat. A good cattery will only breed a queen once every 10 to 12 months. Some catteries unwisely allow their queens to have over 3 litters a year, producing up to 6 kittens or more per breeding. It is extremely difficult for a queen to have multiple litters without the proper rest to regain her weight and strength.

Only the stud males have provided their purrs of contentment when it comes to their personal overbreeding.

Ownership Agreement: This document is also known as a 'Kitten Contract'. When purchasing a purebred feline buyers are informed that the cattery maintains ownership of the feline's breeding rights. When purchasing a kitten the buyer does not maintain any rights to breed their cat. Only the cattery has breeding rights to kittens born within their cattery. Once purchased as a 'pet' the breeder may still own the breeding rights but the purchaser legally owns their feline. A contract is signed in agreement to have the cat altered at the appropriate age. The contract should also stipulate further conditions to protect the kitten such as the buyer will never declaw their cat, will not permit the cat outside access and will provide annual vet checks and vaccinations as required. Contracts vary according to the breeder and the buyer should be careful before signing any documentation if not in agreement with the terms.

Pet Out: This term is used when breeders have decided to give a queen or stud male away to a home where they will be loved and well cared for. It is best to leave the feline with the cattery veterinarian for altering and the new owner to accept the feline after the procedure has been completed. This is an ideal situation for seniors who may wish to have a purebred feline without the work of a kitten. The breeder will have an intimate knowledge of the feline and play matchmaker by successfully placing the cat in the right home. Depending on the circumstances the breeder may request a nominal fee for the cost of altering or simply gift the feline to the new owner.

Pet Quality: Every cattery produces a number of Pet Quality kittens. For example in a litter of four kittens the breeder is considered fortunate if one kitten is of Breeding Quality and three kittens are Pet Quality. Breeders assess their kittens according to the standard as determined by their Cat Association. The closer the kittens meet the standard determines their quality within the breed. Catteries would be unable to survive without the sale of the many Pet Quality kittens produced each breeding season.

Proven Male: When a young male successfully sires a litter, he is known as a 'proven' male.

Purr Name: Every kitten in a litter is given a purr name by its mother. The interesting vocalizations of the mother when summoning her litter for nursing are the individual purr names for each kitten.

When the kittens become older and are able to explore the cattery they will locate quiet areas to sleep. When the mother needs to nurse she will awaken her kittens from their hidden places by 'chirping' loudly and calling each kitten's individual purr name. If a breeder is able to view the sleeping litter it is sometimes possible to distinguish which sounds have been given to each kitten. When a kitten fails to appear the mother will continue to vocalize that baby's purr name in a loud, repetitive 'chirping' series until the kitten responds.

Queen or Dam: A grown female cat is referred to as a queen or dam. This term applies to both pet and breeding female cats, regardless whether they are domestic or purebred.

Raised Lovingly Under Foot: This term signifies that kittens are born and raised in a home environment. Although as a novice Jasmine proudly displayed this term on her business cards, she later removed it. She is no longer comfortable with this term because of the negative reference to 'under foot'. She experienced the misfortune of having a guest accidentally step on a six-week-old kitten. She was forced to end the baby's life herself, as it suffered terribly from the trauma.

After sharing this heartbreaking tragedy with many breeders it was agreed that this description was inappropriate and may draw negative energy into the cattery. Perhaps 'home raised' or 'family raised' would be better terms.

Registered Breeder: In most Cat Associations the breeder is given the same registration number as her cattery. When the cattery name is accepted and registered the breeder submitting the cattery for registration is automatically registered as well.

Registered Cattery: A cattery will be registered when a National 'Cat Association' accepts the breeder's chosen cattery name. Due to the multitude of catteries previously registered in each Association, it may take several attempts to have your unique name accepted.

Your registered cattery name may appear in another Association, however your registered name will remain unique within your own chosen Association. Every kitten born within your cattery will keep your registered cattery name for the duration of their life. While an owner may change the registered name of a feline the originating cattery name can never be changed.

Registered Kitten: When you purchase a purebred kitten from a 'registered cattery', the kitten cannot be registered until you obtain the correct registration forms from the breeder. It then becomes your responsibility to register your kitten.

A nominal registration fee is to be forwarded with the completed forms. The breeder's cattery name is the first name shown on the kitten's registration, followed by the personally chosen name for your kitten. The Association will request that you choose two different names in the unlikely event that another kitten from the same cattery was previously registered with the same name.

Many new kitten owners assume that their feline is registered when purchased. However breeders will not release the registration forms until the kitten has been altered according to the 'Ownership Agreement' contract. Although some buyers assume it is the cattery's responsibility to automatically register their kitten only the owner is able to register and provide the legal name for their purebred. After a feline has been altered the kitten owner will be issued with a 'Certificate of Castration' from the veterinarian. Upon presentation of this document to the breeder the application for individual feline registration will be supplied. When completed these forms are to be forwarded to the Registered Cat Association providing the choice of name
for the feline.

Registered Litter:
Even when a 'sire' (stud male) and 'dam' (queen) are registered with a Cat Association, the resulting litter will only be recognized when the breeder pays a fee and submits the appropriate registration forms.

Litters should be registered approximately two weeks from the time of birth to ensure the health of the litter and to show proof of litter registration when the kittens are viewed. Cat Associations are prompt in acknowledging litter registrations and quickly forward the individual kitten registration slips to the breeder.

Also see **Stud Male** and **Queen**.

Shallow Heat: A queen is said to be experiencing a shallow heat when she is not actively showing all physical aspects of a standard heat cycle. Shallow heats are sometimes displayed at the conclusion of the annual breeding season.

Show Quality or Top Show Quality: Every breeder's desire is to produce the best example of their breed. It takes many years of breeding to produce Show Quality kittens. Further selective breeding incorporating the best compatible bloodlines may eventually yield a Top Show Quality kitten. These kittens, male or female, are rarely sold to other catteries due to the time, high cost and rarity to produce.

Spraying: Male cats spray leaving their individual odor to mark their territory. Some stud males are chronic sprayers while others seldom spray. The spray scent from a male cat is unmistakable. Some 'whole' males are non-sprayers. These precious males bless their catteries by never leaving their personal calling card inside or outside the confines of their nooks.

A female cat may spray urine against walls or furniture during a heat cycle or when overstressed. This sometimes occurs when there is limited space in an overcrowded cattery.

Stud Male or Sire: This term only refers to breeding male cats. Breeding males are incredibly loving but may also be difficult to handle.

To Throw also known as To Throw Better Than Himself or Queen & Studs, How They Throw: These terms are common breeder jargon and refer to the 'quality of kitten' respective males and queens are able to produce. Stud males are sometimes known to Throw Better Than Himself. Such a male has strong bloodlines and may consistently produce a standard of kitten better than he is himself. A male that is not of Top Show Quality when bred with compatible queens may consistently produce kittens that are of Top Show Quality. Such kittens are in demand and often prove quite competitive in the show ring.

When a breeder uses the term How They Throw the reference is to one stud male and one particular breeding queen in the consistency of the show standard of their many litters.

Twice In Once Out: When a queen is a product of an 'out cross breeding' union and is bred back to her father the breeder has adopted the practice of Twice In Once Out. The initial out cross breeding that produced the queen is considered <u>first</u> into the bloodline. The second breeding back to the father is <u>twice</u> into the bloodline. The breeder must leave the gene pool and breed once out to continue producing genetically safe kittens.

The above is an abbreviated explanation of a very complex genetic breeding practice. Greater detail and thorough explanations in simple to understand language of how to accomplish these breeding techniques are explained in Volume 4 of the **Felines by Design** series.

Unproven Male: A young male, not quite ready to breed but purchased with the intention of becoming the cattery's 'stud male' is referred to as 'unproven'. Breeders may keep a promising male to see if they will eventually 'throw better' than their 'sires'. Some of these males are Top Show Quality at birth but their quality may change as they age. Breeders sometimes keep a Top Show Quality male only to realize despite numerous breedings the male will only produce Pet

Quality kittens. A good breeder will usually choose to 'alter' and 'pet out' such a male. Other breeders may follow the unprofessional practice of pawning off this type of male proven or not to a novice breeder.

Whole Cat: An uncastrated cat is also referred to as a whole cat. Male or female, domestic or purebred, whole cats are ruled by their hormones. When your cat is altered, you are blessed with a more secure, non-territorial feline that will readily bond with family members.

Check with your veterinarian regarding the correct age to alter. Queens should be altered prior to their first heat. Males should be altered before they start spraying.

Notes

Notes

Printed in the United Kingdom
by Lightning Source UK Ltd.
111420UKS00001B/161